Travels and Travails

Tourism at Mesa Verde

By
Duane A. Smith
William C. Winkler

Copyright © 2005 by The Durango Herald Small Press

All rights reserved, including the right to reproduce this book
or portions thereof in any form, store in a retrieval system,
or transmit in any form or by any means, electronic, mechanical,
photocopy, recording, or otherwise without permission in writing
from the publisher, except by a reviewer who may
quote brief passages in a review.

ISBN 1-887805-17-6

Authors
Duane A. Smith
William C. Winkler

Mesa Verde Centennial Series Editor
Andrew Gulliford

Content and Copy Editor
Elizabeth A. Green

Design and Layout
Lisa Snider Atchison

Mesa Verde Centennial Series Editorial Committee
Lisa Snider Atchison, Tracey L. Chavis,
Elizabeth A. Green, Andrew Gulliford, Tessy Shirakawa,
Duane A. Smith and Robert Whitson

Printed in Korea

For Robert Lister

teacher, historian, archaeologist

and a mentor/friend

A message from the Superintendent of Mesa Verde National Park

Our centennial celebrates an important moment in Mesa Verde National Park's history. It is an opportunity to share stories of what led to establishment of the park on June 29, 1906, and its designation as a World Heritage Cultural Site in 1978. This is a time to reflect upon its past and share hopes and visions for the next 100 years.

As Mesa Verde National Park nears its 100th birthday, it is important to remember that the archaeological sites it protects have been here far longer. Their survival is a credit to the skilled Ancestral Puebloan masons who created them 700 to 1600 years ago.

Following the Puebloan people's migration south to the Rio Grande area around 1300, the Utes continued to occupy the Mesa Verde area. They remain today and were responsible for the protection and preservation of Mesa Verde prior to its establishment as a national park. The park and the American public owe much to all these surviving indigenous people.

More than 100 years before its establishment as a national park, non-native people began exploring and documenting the archaeological sites at Mesa Verde, including Spanish explorers, geologists, ranchers, miners, photographers, naturalists, and archaeologists. They shared the story of fantastic stone cities in the cliffs, attracting more and more visitors to the area.

Prior to 1914, the 25-mile trek from Mancos Canyon to Spruce Tree House took an entire day, traveling the first 15 miles by wagon and the next 10 miles on foot or by horseback. This included a nearly vertical climb to the top of Chapin Mesa. Today more than one-half million people visit Mesa Verde National Park each year – a considerable increase over the 100 visitors documented in 1906.

"Leaving the past in place" is just one of the unique ideas pioneered at Mesa Verde. In 1908, when archaeology mainly consisted of collecting artifacts for distant museums, Jesse Walter Fewkes repaired, but did not rebuild, Spruce Tree House for visitation. He documented the excavation and created a small museum to house its artifacts. That tradition is continued today and Mesa Verde is recognized worldwide as a leader in non-invasive archaeology – studying and documenting sites without shovels to disturb the past. With the involvement of the 24 tribes affiliated with Mesa Verde and ongoing research, we continue to learn more about the stories that Mesa Verde National Park preserves.

Our centennial will celebrate 100 years of preservation and honor all who have gone before us. This centennial book series was created to tell some of their stories, of discovery, travel, transportation, archaeology, fire and tourism. These stories have contributed to our national heritage and reinforce why we must continue to preserve and protect this national treasure for future generations.

Enjoy the celebration. Enjoy the book series. Enjoy your national park.

– Larry T. Wiese

About the Mesa Verde Museum Association

Mesa Verde Museum Association (MVMA) is a nonprofit, 501 (c) 3 organization, authorized by Congress, established in 1930, and incorporated in 1960. MVMA was the second "cooperating association" formed in the United States after the Yosemite Association. Since its inception, the museum association has provided information that enables visitors to more fully appreciate the cultural and natural resources in Mesa Verde National Park and the southwestern United States. Working under a memorandum of agreement with the National Park Service, the association assists and supports various research activities, interpretive and education programs, and visitor services at Mesa Verde National Park.

A Board of Directors sets policy and provides guidance for the association. An Executive Director assures mission goals are met, strengthens partnerships, and manages publishing, education, and membership program development. A small year-round staff of five, along with more than 15 seasonal employees, operates four sales outlets in Mesa Verde National Park and a bookstore in Cortez, Colorado. The association carries nearly 600 items, the majority of which are produced by outside vendors. MVMA currently publishes approximately 40 books, videos, and theme-related items, and more than 15 trail guides.

Since 1996 MVMA has been a charter partner in the Plateau Journal, a semiannual interpretive journal covering the people and places of the Colorado Plateau. In addition, the association has been a driving force in the Peaks, Plateaus & Canyons Association (PPCA), a region-wide conference of nonprofit interpretive associations. PPCA promotes understanding and protection of the Colorado Plateau through the publication of joint projects that are not feasible for smaller associations.

Mesa Verde Museum Association is also a longtime member of the Association of Partners for Public Lands (APPL). This national organization of nonprofit interpretive associations provides national representation with our land management partners and highly specialized training opportunities for board and staff.

Since 1930 the association has donated more than $2 million in cash contributions, interpretive services, and educational material to Mesa Verde National Park. MVMA's goal is to continue enhancing visitor experience through its products and services, supporting vital park programs in interpretation, research and education.

Visit the online bookstore at mesaverde.org and learn more about Mesa Verde National Park's centennial celebration at mesaverde2006.org. Contact MVMA offices for additional information at: telephone 970-529-4445; write P.O. Box 38, Mesa Verde National Park, CO 81330; or email info@mesaverde.org.

 Center of Southwest Studies

The Center of Southwest Studies

The Center of Southwest Studies on the campus of Fort Lewis College in Durango, Colorado, serves as a museum and a research facility, hosts public programs, and strengthens an interdisciplinary Southwest college curriculum. Fort Lewis College offers a four-year degree in Southwest Studies with minors in Native American Studies and Heritage Preservation. The Center includes a 4,400-square-foot gallery, the Robert Delaney Research Library, a 100-seat lyceum, and more than 10,000 square feet of collections storage. The new $8 million Center of Southwest Studies building is unique among four-year public colleges in the West, because the facility houses the departments of Southwest Studies and Anthropology, and the Office of Community Services, which helps Four Corners communities with historic preservation and cultural resource planning.

The Colorado Commission on Higher Education has recognized the Center of Southwest Studies as a "program of excellence" in state-funded higher education. Recent gifts to the Center include the $2.5 million Durango Collection ®, which features more than eight hundred years of southwestern weavings from Pueblo, Navajo and Hispanic cultures.

The goal of the Center is to become the intellectual heart of Durango and the Southwest and to provide a variety of educational and research opportunities for students, residents, scholars and visitors. Strengths in the Center's collections of artifacts include Ancestral Puebloan ceramic vessels, more than 500 textiles and dozens of southwestern baskets. The Center's holdings, which focus on the Four Corners region, include more than 8,000 artifacts, 20,000 volumes, numerous periodicals, and 500 special collections dating from prehistory to the present and with an emphasis on southwestern archaeology, maps, and original documents. These collections include nearly two linear miles of manuscripts, unbound printed materials, more than 7,000 rolls of microfilm (including about 3,000 rolls of historic Southwest region newspapers), 600 oral histories, and 200,000 photographs. Contact the Center at 970-247-7456 or visit the Center's website at swcenter.fortlewis.edu. The Center hosts tours, educational programs, a speakers' series, and changing exhibits throughout the year.

Center of SW Studies website: http://swcenter.fortlewis.edu

About the publisher

The publisher for the Mesa Verde Centennial Series is the Ballantine family of Durango and the Durango Herald Small Press. The Ballantine family moved to the Four Corners region in 1952 when it purchased the *Durango Herald* newspaper.

Durango has a magnificent setting, close to the Continental Divide, the 13,000-foot San Juan Mountains, and the 500,000-acre Weminuche Wilderness. The Four Corners region encompasses the juncture of Colorado, Utah, Arizona, and New Mexico, the only place in the nation where four state borders meet. Residents can choose to ski one day in the San Juans and hike the next day in the wilderness canyons of southeast Utah. This land of mountains and canyons, deserts and rivers is home to diverse Native American tribes including the Southern Utes, Ute Mountain Utes, Jicarilla Apache, Hopi, Zuni, and the Navajo, whose 17 million-acre nation sprawls across all four states. The Four Corners is situated on the edge of the Colorado Plateau, which has more national forests, national parks, national monuments, and wilderness areas than anywhere else on earth.

Writing and editing the newspaper launched countless family expeditions to Ancestral Puebloan sites in the area, including spectacular Mesa Verde National Park, the world's first park set aside for the preservation of cultural resources in 1906 to honor America's indigenous peoples. The Ballantine family, through the *Durango Herald* and the *Cortez Journal,* have been strong supporters of Mesa Verde National Park and Fort Lewis College.

Arthur and Morley Ballantine started the planning for the Center of Southwest Studies at Fort Lewis College in 1964 with a $10,000 gift. In 1994 Morley began the Durango Herald Small Press, which publishes books of local and regional interest. The Press is proud to be a part of the 100th birthday celebration for Mesa Verde National Park.

Durango Herald Small Press website: www.theheraldstore.com

Table of Contents

Foreword XI

Prologue:
First Tourists Arrive XII

Chapter 1: 1870s-1900s Wetherills "Discover,"
Visitors Arrive, Women Save 3

Chapter 2: Three Little Towns and Tourism 19

Chapter 3: 1907-1919 Travails for the Timid Tourist 39

Chapter 4: Tourists by the Carload .69

Chapter 5: Postcards Welcome You to Mesa Verde 93

Chapter 6: Founding of the Mesa Verde Company 107

Chapter 7: Old Problems, New Problems 1940s-1970s 121

Chapter 8: The Roger Hall and William Winkler Years 145

Chapter 9: The Fabulous Four Corners 1980s-2005 167

Epilogue:
Place of National and International Interest 179

FOREWORD

Mesa Verde National Park was established on June 29, 1906, by Congress. Approximately 10 years later the National Park Service was created by Congress to manage the properties that had been set aside. Their mandate was to "protect, preserve, and provide for future enjoyment by the people." Nothing in the acts stipulated that they should *promote visitation*. And so the tradition began; the National Park Service would provide the infrastructure while a concessioner would build and promote visitor facilities.

The beginning of tourism in Mesa Verde is difficult to identify. We know the Ancestral Puebloans had trade connections with neighboring people. Scarlet macaw feathers, sea shells, turquoise and pottery all testify to this. The "moccasin telegraph" existed and so did the need to accommodate the travelers. Later, Dominguez and Escalante passed nearby in August of 1776. They too were "tourists" of sorts.

For many years, Mesa Verde was unique among national parks, the only one set aside for the works of man. Interpretation had to be different than in natural history parks. Understanding the cultural history of Ancestral Puebloans was, and is, essential for park visitors.

Through the years, superintendents have come and gone more frequently than concessioners. As a result, the concessioners' longevity and continuity of work in the park has conferred a stewardship responsibility on concessions operators. Tourism is about people, and businesses that provide visitor services are in "the people business."

The experiences, views and observations we present in this book are based on 45 years of hands-on activities in Mesa Verde. Add to that the 22 years we've continued to closely follow what has gone on in the park since our work there stopped, and our association with Mesa Verde spans more than two-thirds of the park's 100 years. It is, we believe, a remarkable story.

– **William C. Winkler with Merrie Hall Winkler**

PROLOGUE

FIRST TOURISTS ARRIVE

BY DUANE A. SMITH

Surrounded by towering mountains, lonely deserts, hulking mesas, and deep river canyons, southwestern Colorado and its Four Corners neighbor states long remained an isolated, unknown region to the onrushing European/American settlers. To be sure, prehistoric Puebloan people had lived there, followed by Utes and Navajos who wandered, planted a little, and hunted throughout much of the area.

Then came some newcomers, the Spanish, who settled along the Rio Grande and penetrated northward looking for gold, trade, and converts to their Catholic faith. They left behind melodic names for rivers, mountains, mesas, and prominent points. Nonetheless, they did not settle or permanently convert many to their religion. Legends and lost mines came in their wake, tantalizing generations to follow.

While Americans declared their independence from England in 1776, two determined Franciscan friars, Francisco Dominguez and Silvestre Escalante, left Santa Fe on an expedition in search of a route to the new Spanish settlements along the Pacific coast of modern California. Young Americans looked west, too, but they would wait awhile to venture across the wide Missouri. Why would they travel so far when more promising land beckoned closer by?

> "THE 19TH CENTURY DAWNED WITH A YOUNG, VIBRANT UNITED STATES FAR TO THE EAST ACROSS THE MISSISSIPPI RIVER, AND A DECAYING SPANISH EMPIRE RIGHT NEXT DOOR, IN EVERY DIRECTION BUT NORTH."

The tiring, tedious walk or ride from the nearest settlement may have colored many an impression of the future Four Corners. Escalante and those that followed him encountered canyons, deserts, sagebrush plains, rivers, mesas, and, depending on the route, mountains. Lack of water proved another hindrance, particularly from the south.

In early August, as the Spanish friars traveled through southwestern Colorado, Escalante recorded his impressions of this land in his journal. He reported sagebrush stretches with "little pasturage," and on August 14, "a troublesome stretch of sagebrush." Then the party encountered a "tall and craggy canyon." Never completely discouraged, he also wrote that they had passed through "leafy tree growth with good pasturage." Scattered about this vast land, there existed some potential. Westerners a century later would see more than Escalante wrote of in his journal.

The 19th century dawned with a young, vibrant United States far to the east across the Mississippi River, and a decaying Spanish empire right next door, in every direction but north. The last years of peace and quiet settled over this land.

Beavers, for untold centuries, had contentedly splashed and constructed dams and homes in mountain streams. Such tranquility came to an end though, when beaver hats, coats, and a variety of other beaver apparel came into fashion in the courts of Europe and homes of America. French, English, Indian, and finally American trappers crisscrossed the land to the east, searching out beaver for more than two centuries. Now, after the war of 1812, they ventured into the central Rockies.

Trappers out of Taos and Santa Fe found the San Juans a tempting hunting ground, but not much farther south of them, where the climate turned too warm and the water too scarce to maintain a large number of beavers. The few beavers living south of the mountains developed pelts that were adapted to hotter seasons and therefore less luxurious than those coming from colder climes.

Still, some trappers wandered through the region, including William Becknell, who had helped open the Santa Fe trade in 1820 and in so doing changed the destiny of this region. Four years later in the winter of 1824-25, he set up winter quarters near, if not in, Mesa Verde. In a letter to the Franklin *Missouri Intelligencer*, June 25, 1825, he wrote this description: "The country here is poor and only timbered with pine and cedar. We suffered every misery incident to such an enterprise in the winter season, such as hunger and cold."

His letter further "enhanced" the image of the region. "Out of food. The flesh of a very lean horse, which we were constrained to break our fast with, was at this, pronounced excellent." It got worse. "...we subsisted two days on soup made of a raw hide we had reserved for sealing our moccasins. The young men employed by me had seen better days and had never before been supperless in bed nor missed a wholesome and substantial meal at the regular family hour." They all persevered, as Becknell explained, because they would not "give odds to die."

In 1848, following the conclusion of the Mexican War, this region became part of the United States. Eleven years later an expedition led by Major John Macomb ventured into the area. Geologist John Newberry climbed to the top of Mesa Verde, enjoyed the breathtaking view but observed, "To us, however, as well as to all the civilized world, it was a terra incognita ..."

Much like Escalante, the San Juan exploring expedition squeezed in favorable comments. For example, a report stated that near to the "mountains it is pretty well timbered," amid less favorable descriptions such as, "The country lying between the Mancos and Dolores [rivers] is generally dry and sterile." Fascinated by the relics of "former residents," they could only note, "it is now utterly deserted." The river valleys, with their watered bottom lands, appeared "very fertile," surrounded by wide intervals "covered with sage-bushes and soap-plant."

Truthfully, there seemed little to attract people to this secluded corner of the United States. There always existed the hope that something would be found, but reports so far had been less than flattering. Many more promising opportunities existed elsewhere in the West.

So it looked, as Americans entered that epic upheaval they called the Civil War, or the war of "Northern aggression," depending on one's viewpoint. It scarcely touched the Four Corners land, although it surged nearby in the Rio Grande Valley.

Meanwhile, the Pike's Peak gold rush brought the hopeful and the expectant to the mountains. Briefly, a gold boom flourished. The region gained a name, Colorado, but the boom soon passed, and depression sat dismally down on optimism and prospects. The 1860s were not a decade to be fondly remembered by these early Coloradans.

The end of the war, the Industrial Revolution transforming America, the search for gold and silver, and the arrival of adventuresome, resolute people would soon bring changes to this lonely, isolated land. It would never be the same again.

– **Duane A. Smith**

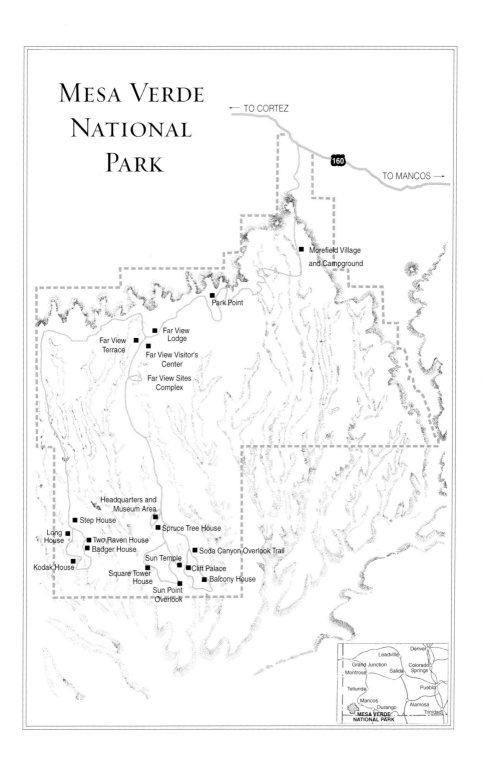

I

1870s-1900s
Wetherills "Discover,"
Visitors Arrive, Women Save

By Duane A. Smith

The 1870s found Colorado gaining railroad connections, achieving statehood, and surpassing California and Nevada to emerge as number one in mining in the United States. Even isolated southwestern Colorado made progress. Prospectors and miners ventured into the San Juans, and permanent settlement followed. Animas City took root in the Animas River valley, and the tiny mining camp of Parrott City claimed a spot at the mouth of La Plata Canyon.

Mining, which had brought people to the Pike's Peak region in 1859, now lured them into southwestern Colorado in the 1870s. Prospectors ranged high into the San Juan Mountains where they found the going difficult over the lofty passes, including the well-named Stony Pass. Nor were supply points very close. Abiquiu and Santa Fe, New Mexico, and Oro City and Cañon City, Colorado, all required a week's journey each way through some rugged terrain. Still, people came, beckoned by the often irresistible but ill-fated lure of gold.

VISITORS FROM RAIN-BLESSED, HUMID, TREE-DOTTED LANDS USUALLY HAD TROUBLE UNDERSTANDING OR QUICKLY ADAPTING TO THE MORE SEMI-ARID ENVIRONMENT.

Visitors, too, started to come to see the "ruins of the ancients," as word drifted out of what was being found in some canyons and river valleys. Photographer William Henry Jackson arrived, in September 1874, to take the first photographs of sites in Mancos Canyon and as far west as McElmo Canyon. Meanwhile, he traveled completely around Mesa Verde and missed the ruins on top. Readers of the *New York Tribune* (November 3) learned all about his adventures and those mysterious ruins. Visitors to the 1876 Centennial Exposition in Philadelphia could view a Jackson model "of one of the curious and interesting villages of the ancient Aztecs of southern Colorado."

Other stories about the region's ancient remains followed, including one that appeared in Denver's *Rocky Mountain News* (November 25, 1877), comparing "these majestic ruins" favorably "with the ancient magnificence of Rome and Greece." Emma Hardacre, writing in 1878, was not impressed with what a tourist had to overcome to reach these intriguing ruins. While she persevered, Emma warned her readers about what lay ahead. The remote location, the nearest railroad being 200 to 300 miles distant, forced one to cross a "waterless, trackless desert, dotted by sage-brush and stunted greasewood enlivened by rattlesnakes, horned toads, and tarantulas." She concluded that the triangle area of 600 square miles bounded by the Rio Mancos,

La Plata, and Rio San Juan "does not contain a drop of water."

Visitors from rain-blessed, humid, tree-dotted lands usually had trouble understanding or quickly adapting to the more semi-arid environment. Despite such negative views, interest grew in southwestern Colorado in a variety of ways – mining, farming, ranching, urban development, and visiting those mysterious "Aztec" sites.

Colorado writer and booster Frank Fossett wrote in the 1876 edition of his *Colorado* that this country had remained *terra incognita* until very recently when mining prospects finally opened it. It might have been unknown, but that now was changing, and Fossett took time to praise the "rich valleys" of the Animas, La Plata, Mancos, and San Juan rivers. He also pointed out to his readers that this region contained the "dead cities of the ancient Aztecs."

A variety of conflicting views appeared in print about this land and its potential. In 1877, William Morgan visited the Mancos Valley, which had been lately "settled by a few American farmers," on his way to see a cliff house. He described neighboring Thompson Park as "one of the prettiest in the Rocky Mountain region," and in the Mancos Valley he praised the irrigation cultivation that had just been inaugurated.

Quite the contrary came Henry Gannett's impression, a view that must have startled many readers.

> From the southern and western slopes of the San Juan Mountains, in southwestern Colorado, stretches far to the south and west a strange country. It is a country of plateaus and canons – of plateaus whose surfaces are flat and unbroken for miles on miles; as far as one can see, the country presents a monotonous level, but is cut here and there by deep, almost impassable, canons. As we recede from the mountains, these plateaus, which are there covered with pinon pine and sage, become more sterile, and finally vegetation ceases, except in isolated spots, and the surface is bare rock or drifting sand – a very Sahara.

This "very Sahara" did have oases, the rivers running out of the mountains. To Gannett, the water in the Rio Mancos, La Plata, Animas and other rivers left the mountains as "clear, beautiful streams." Even that did not last, as the sparkling water soon became "discolored, alkaline, and in a few miles disappears. The dry atmosphere and the parched earth have absorbed it, and a dry canon alone remains to mock the thirsty traveler." He thought in the early spring the streams might for a "short time – a week or two, perhaps, each be filled with a rushing torrent." The armchair reader back east would have gained, at best, reservations about this land of mysterious ancient people. How could they possibly have lived there?

George Crofutt, in his 1885 *Grip-Sack Guide of Colorado*, objected to the desert image. This country, he wrote, "is no means a total desert as some writers represent." Like Fossett before him, he praised the streams, their grass-covered meadows, and their rich bottom lands. This debate, desert vs. garden land, would continue for generations.

Attention might be called to the area, but it did not lessen the trials and tribulations of trying to reach the mines, valleys, and ruins. This "remote corner of Colorado" remained out of the way. That was fine with its long-time residents, the Utes, who were not happy in the least about intruders overrunning their lands. They did sign the Brunot agreement (1873) that opened the vast mountainous region from the eastern San Juan Mountains to nearly Utah, but tensions lingered nonetheless.

It proved just a matter of time before those tensions exploded, which they did in 1879 in what Coloradans called the "Ute War." In response to the killing of agent Nathan Meeker and 11 other men at the White River Reservation agency in northwestern Colorado, the federal government removed almost all the Utes. Only the Southern Utes remained on their lands stretching across southern Colorado and neighboring New Mexico, for nearly 100 miles in front of the oncoming settlers.

Because of these troubles, the army established a military post, Fort Lewis, in western La Plata County. Reassured by the military presence, urban settlers, farmers, and ranchers arrived in the various river valleys to carve out homesteads or settle in towns. The San Juan miners and mining camps provided a readily available market for their products, produce, and animals.

The first real break in their isolation came with the arrival in the Animas Valley of the Denver & Rio Grande Railroad in 1881, on its way to tap the mines in and around Silverton, high in the mountains to the north. A dispute with farming community Animas City regarding assistance to the railroad had led to the founding of Durango the year before. Quickly, the new "metropolis" became the largest community in southwestern Colorado. More than 2,000 inhabitants soon crowded into a sweeping bend of the Animas River. Almost overnight, it became the transportation, business, banking, social, and commercial center for the region. Both the railroad and its town would be essential keys to overcoming the isolation and transportation obstacles that had so long plagued the area. Two miles away, Animas City, which misjudged its importance, languished.

Mining attracted permanent settlement to the mountains, and other settlers arrived in the warmer river valleys where lower elevation created longer growing seasons. Lured by the mining markets, abundant water, and now better transportation, these urban and agricultural pioneers came and stayed. Soon too, their tiny villages dotted the landscape, including Durango, Animas City, and Mancos, and later Bayfield and Cortez.

Little Mancos provided the starting point for the story of the "discovery" of Mesa Verde. Among the settlers along the Mancos River was the Benjamin Wetherill family. Unlike some of their neighbors, these Quaker ranchers got along well with the Southern Utes, whose reservation lay just

Mesa Verde National Park

The Wetherill brothers, from left, Al, Win, Richard, Clayton and John

down the canyon from their ranch. The Utes allowed the Wetherills to winter their cattle in the shelter of the Mancos Canyon, and from those winter camps some of the sons rode into the canyons stretching into Mesa Verde, looking for stray cattle. What they found led to the adventure of a lifetime.

It would not be easy initially. William Henry Jackson described his difficulties during his earlier trip. The "thick-matted jungle of undergrowth, tall reedy grass, willows, and thorny bushes, all interlaced and entwined by tough and wiry grape-vines bordering its bank upon either one side or the other" hindered his party in the main Mancos canyon. In the smaller canyons fingering into Mesa Verde a worse mess awaited anyone attempting to enter their depths.

Richard Wetherill and his brother-in-law Charlie Mason were searching for stray cattle or on a "cruise of exploration," (stories vary) on a December day in 1888 when they peered across a canyon and saw a remarkable sight. Mason recalled, "from the rim of the canon we had our first view of Cliff Palace. To me this is the grandest view of all among the ancient ruins of the Southwest."

They spent several hours picking up souvenirs, then excitedly returned to their camp.

In the following weeks, the Wetherills made more visits and gathered a collection of relics. These they displayed in Durango, where they realized, much to their amazement, that people would pay to see what they had found. That turning point quickly changed people's attitude and behavior toward the ruins scattered across the region. Eventually the Wetherills took their show on the road, ultimately reaching Denver, where they sold the collection to the Colorado Historical Society.

With money to be made, the new "gold" rush hastened ahead with word quickly spreading beyond the Four Corners states. Curious visitors started to arrive at the Wetherills' Alamo Ranch, wanting to visit those intriguing ruins. With the Wetherill boys guiding trips into the canyon sites, these visitors generated additional family income. For an economically slumbering Mancos valley, this bonanza came at the right moment. Other local folk were not about to let the opportunity pass.

Mesa Verde National Park

Gustaf Nordenskiöld

A young Swedish scholar, Gustaf Nordenskiöld, arrived in July 1891. He excavated and photographed a hall-of-fame-worth of the sites and left with a collection of artifacts. Some Durangoans protested against a foreigner taking their "American" relics, but could do nothing about it. No laws existed prohibiting such activities. Two years later, in 1893, Nordenskiöld published the first study of the by then much better known and intriguing Mesa Verde.

More attention came when one of the Wetherill collections emerged as a popular attraction at the 1893 World's Columbian Exposition (Chicago World's Fair). The exhibit almost outshone "Little Egypt" (an "infamous" belly dancer, according to some), that new taste treat cotton candy, long-distance phone calls, and the "world-renowned" Buffalo Bill's Wild West Show.

> One enters a cavernous portal to find a representation (on a scale of one-tenth the actual size) of the wondrous and long-deserted cliff-dwellings of the Mancos Canon Colorado. With an excellent exactitude the H. Jay Smith Exploring Co. have reproduced the finest of the cliff-dwellings, constructed rocky trails for the adventurous to traverse, and arranged a valuable collection of cliff relics for the inspection of the scientist, student, or curious. Admission, 25 cents: catalogue, 10 cents.

Richard Wetherill himself journeyed to the big city to beguile exhibit visitors with firsthand accounts of the "discovery" and the region. To preserve decorum and Victorian sensibilities, a separate room contained the "mummies" that had been found. These had proved a big hit in Colorado, while at the same time raising concerns about their appropriateness for all people, especially the young and women of all ages. Seeing those desiccated bodies with the hair and skin still clinging to them did not seem proper for genteel Victorian women.

All this publicity brought a steady and slowly growing number of tourists to the Alamo Ranch and Mancos. Fortunately, getting there had become somewhat easier. The Rio Grande Southern Railroad had been constructed (1890-1891) in a sweeping loop from Durango to Ridgway far to the north. Mancos folk proudly pointed to their brand new depot, eagerly awaited those travelers sure to come, and planned for the irrefutable coming prosperity.

Considering earlier travel accounts, a new era had arrived. After riding the Denver & Rio Grande from Denver to Durango, the next morning one boarded the Rio Grande Southern. Departing at Mancos within hours, the tourist would be only a day's ride from the heart of Mesa Verde, a mere two days after leaving Denver.

Hoping to capitalize on that fact, the Rio Grande Southern promptly pointed out the ease, comfort, and speed with which it took visitors to the "ruins of the ancients." That might be, but people still experienced troubles reaching their destination for a variety of reasons, from inaccurate expectations to poor roads. Nor were some of their impressions of the region overly flattering. People reading earlier and current accounts could come to an obvious conclusion that only the adventuresome, or foolish, would venture into the seemingly Godforsaken land.

Frederick Chapin, who would have a mesa named after him, on the contrary found the region a "wonderland." He arrived before the Rio Grande Southern and wrote a narrative of his trip from Durango to Mancos. Initially, Chapin found it difficult to secure information, but he finally did and rented a "two-horse conveyance." Off he and a companion went, already harboring an idea of what they were going to encounter.

> The drive was a very interesting one. Leaving Durango at 7:55 A. M., we passed through a country of coal-mines, and reached the top of the mesa at 9:30 A. M. ... At 11:30 o'clock we put up at Dick's ranch, where we rested our horses for an hour and twenty minutes, and had our dinner. Around this ranch are very tall pine-trees. The proprietor raises about forty tons of hay annually, and crops of oats, wheat and potatoes. These facts all entertained us, for we had supposed we were about to enter a semi-desert.

> An hour beyond Dick's ranch we came to the edge of a mesa and could look down upon the valley of Mancos. It was a great surprise. Instead of a parched and arid region, we were looking upon a beautiful land where great fields of golden grain covered hillside and valley. Hastening forward we reached the Wetherill ranch at 3:40.

Even if it did take Chapin a day to travel to Mancos over country roads, it was a faster pace and in more comfort than a traveler of 15 years before could have achieved. The railroad quickly eliminated the buggy or horseback trip from Durango. After enjoying the passing scenery of mountains, valleys and mesas, the visitor arrived with ease at the Mancos station. There the Wetherills, or somebody else, would take them to the Alamo Ranch. It would not be long, however, before competitors also offered tours.

Their trials were not over once visitors reached Mesa Verde. Echoing earlier comments, F. H. Newell, chief hydrographer of the U.S. Geological Survey, depicted the lowlands around Mesa Verde as "arid and almost desolate." After "laboriously" climbing to the top, he found that traveling "along the top of these ridges is easy, as the surface is smooth. Numerous cattle trails wind in and out among the trees, and on horseback the ground can be covered as rapidly as the rider can dodge the stiff-pointed, dead, lower branches of the trees." However, to go from canyon to canyon, or down to examine a ruin, proved "almost impossible to make progress. Reaching the edge of a precipice, the explorer wanders up or down until by chance he finds a place where the rock has been broken down, and on reaching the bottom of the valley he must again search perhaps for miles for an opportunity to climb out."

William Birdsall, who toured Mesa Verde in 1891, concurred with earlier assessments. He found the canyon bottoms filled with "tall, coarse grasses, rushes, sage-brush, tangled vines, willow and cottonwood." He felt the views seen while journeying through the canyons "soon become monotonous from the continued repetition of the greater features. We pass promontory after promontory, canon after canon, which so much resemble each other that the mind, failing to keep preceding variations before it, become bewildered and fatigued. Again, the mesa, to the uninitiated, is a perfect maze."

Visitors all rode in via the Mancos Canyon and up narrow trails onto the mesa. Some sightseers found these trails scary, the heights dizzying, and the steep slopes petrifying. One of the worst was the "Crinkle Edge" trail, which gained a reputation to rival the later, better known Knife Edge road. After traveling to the ruins, Palmer Henderson morbidly told his readers that getting lost was easy without guides on these "fearful trails." It would "be the best method for a suicide who didn't wish his family to suspect the death was premeditated." Once they safely arrived, these 1890s tourists typically camped out around what today is known as Spruce Tree House, where they would, within a few years, find primitive cabin accommodations.

Fred Cowling described the adventure as being over "rather rough trails." Only a "few tourists were accustomed to such extended riding under such conditions." His party traveled over the sagebrush Mancos Valley to a trail going up the north side of Mesa Verde where they climbed to near the base of Point Lookout, then turned sharply left. There they followed the "general trail" along the upper end of the canyons with sweeping views of the Montezuma Valley. They camped overnight, at what the Wetherills called Soda Spring, before going on to the ruins.

It could be dangerous, however. At least Alice Henderson thought so. She warned her readers to engage guides, "a trip through that unsurveyed, waterless country without them would be suicide." One must carry water and give up "washing as a luxury." The "alkali water takes off what little skin the pinyons leave." Not finished, she drove home yet another familiar warning. The visitor had to ride great distances "over fearful trails, and up and down mountains, trails hard to find, but easy to lose."

Victorian women faced another worry, an emotional one which threatened to besmirch their reputations. Going alone to see the ruins with a group of men was a scandalous proposition. Therefore, high school age Mancos girls found a new occupation. While one woman alone risked damaging her honor, two women provided "respectability." Also, as Effie Eldredge recounted, dresses would never do for riding on a horse. To maintain decorum, bloomers (pants), or overalls, were required. The "ladies were embarrassed by the thought of those ridiculous overalls," she pointed out, "and they waited until the last minute to put them on. They retired into the sage brush, changed, and giggled over being so attired."

Tourists were coming, a business launched, and the routine established (a day's ride in, a day or two to visit sites, then another out of Mesa Verde). Slowly growing Mancos, population 383 in 1900, found itself with a pleasant economic windfall as the self-proclaimed gateway to Mesa Verde. The Wetherills, meanwhile, basked in the glory of being the "discoverers" and the most learned locals regarding these mysterious ancient peoples. With a great deal of pride the *Mancos Times* (January 5, 1894) called the famed Alamo Ranch a "mecca for tourists," a "summer haven of rest and enjoyment." With such benefits and a visit to the ruins as well, what more could a sojourner ask?

All this activity and rummaging about the cliff dwellings raised concerns in some people's minds. Even before the Wetherills and the "rush" of the 1890s, Denver's *Weekly Tribune-Republican* (December 16, 1886) worried about the remains along the Rio Mancos. The editor recommended that Congress "set apart that canon as a public park." Why? "These ruins which have endured through many ages now are in danger of destruction." From what? The "vandals of modern civilization," the editor accused, concluding, "it is for this reason that Congress should provide for their preservation, or else turn them over to the State in order that it may preserve them." Nothing came of his forward looking idea at that time.

State and local pride, and redemption, underlay this sudden preservation interest. Newness did not breed respect. "Colorado is looked upon as crude and new. But in the Canon of the Rio Mancos there are ruins which are so old that in comparison with them the oldest buildings of the East seem but as the work of yesterday." So much for easterners looking down their noses at upstart westerners and their "pretensions." Easterners might give "reverential care" to the preservation of "relics of an age almost within living memory." Colorado could do them one better!

The threat to the ruins, however, proved real and did not die. It only increased as the years passed. Newell, for one, understood this and closed his 1898 article with apprehension.

> It is a matter of regret that these interesting ruins are not being preserved, as even from a commercial aspect they would have an ever-increasing value to that part of the State in attracting tourists from all over the world. In spite of all the difficulties of access, it is estimated that at present 75 parties a year visit the more important of these cliff-houses. It might be practicable to construct a wagon road [into the mesa], but no steps of this kind should be taken to facilitate travel until ample protection is provided to prevent the defacing and injury of the buildings by careless visitors.

Right on all counts, Newell anticipated the future. Fortunately, as he wrote, some of those changes loomed.

The move to preserve the ruins came from an unexpected direction, women. In post-Civil War America, women were slowly breaking out of the traditional mold of wife and mother. To the shock of many men, some "radicals" even pushed for the right to vote. At the same time people flocked to the Mesa Verde exhibit at the World's Fair, Colorado became the first state to grant women an electoral voice. To the amazement of many, Colorado men voted yes on the question.

Women were also involved in saving George Washington's old home, Mount Vernon, in entering the business world (thanks to the typewriter), promoting prohibition, fostering the Chautauqua movement, and a host of other activities. Most fair-sized communities had women's clubs. Here middle- and upper-class members involved themselves with lectures, discussions, book reports, fundraising, and eventually social activism beyond the churches where they had so long been active. State and national organizations linked them together.

Still, it was surprising that women braved southwestern Colorado's isolation and the travel problems to push for a national park to preserve the

Denver Public Library

Virginia Donaghe McClurg

ruins. That idea, in itself, proved novel. The first national park, Yellowstone, had been set aside to preserve natural beauty and features, as did those that followed. Making Mesa Verde a park meant preserving a cultural and historic site. The women who deserved credit for seeing that need, leading the fight, and conceiving the park idea came from Colorado Springs, Virginia McClurg.

Several factors merged in the issue – the problems of isolation, regional image, tourism, travel, and preservation. While Virginia McClurg and her supporters set out to solve only one, preservation, they ended up encountering them all. Before they finished, each would be discussed at least, several were partially worked out, and one was resolved.

Her interest in the ruins first brought McClurg to Mancos as a reporter. She quickly found out about some of the problems. The attractive, fashionably plump young woman arrived "in a freighter's wagon, seated on a vinegar barrel," the only transportation available. "Wet, weary and uncomfortable," McClurg remained determined to visit some ruins. A hastily improvised bed in the school house served as her room in this day and time before tourists often visited Mancos. Unfortunately, the Southern Utes – at the moment upset over the encroachment of their white neighbors – seemed to be threatening a war or perhaps an attack. At least Virginia remembered it in that fashion. Finally, as she claimed, she explored several small ruins with an escort from nearby Fort Lewis. Despite all her travail, a lifelong interest had been born.

She returned and journeyed into the Mancos Canyon to see those "wonderful buried cities." McClurg encountered another problem that would bedevil visitors, lack of water. Alkaline pools provided no relief, so her party dug in the sand to find water. Nothing daunted her, and after her 1889 marriage, with her husband's support, she launched her crusade to save the ruins.

Public apathy and ignorance confronted McClurg from the first. Nevertheless, she quickly gained backing and would not be deterred. From the early 1890s, until the successful creation of the national park, she campaigned with lectures, stereopticon shows, articles, money-raising, and political lobbying. With a martyr's dedication, McClurg pushed ahead. "The Cliff Palace is the prey of the spoiler," she warned, soon it "will be too late to guard these monuments." She intended for women to act "...as custodians of specific ruins while the matter of national preservation" was pending in Washington.

McClurg gained valuable allies, including the equally talented and determined Lucy Peabody, who contributed valuable political connections in Washington, D.C., and Colorado. Washington, however, appeared too slow so she tried a different tack. In an effort to secure a lease on the ruins, McClurg met with Ignacio and other leaders of the Ute Mountain Utes, the Southern Utes having divided into two bands. In that division, the Ute Mountain Utes had gained the western part of the old reservation where most of the ruins were found. The women eventually got a lease signed, only to find out the federal government would not allow citizens to sign private treaties.

Following a Ute meeting, McClurg toured Mesa Verde and commented in an interview about the beauty of the season. "Oh, if I could but paint for you the glories of the Mesa Verde in its autumn dress of

Lucy Peabody

gold and crimson." Mesa Verde had more to offer than simply ancient ruins.

Peabody and McClurg organized the Colorado Cliff Dwellings Association with chapters in four other states. Joined by women's clubs, they lobbied Congress. Peabody was especially helpful with the effort. With her capital connections and experience, she "left no stone unturned." Behind these two women stood a loyal, hardworking cadre of women. They all, in their own way, made contributions.

Their goals now, as the century turned, focused on two fronts – educational work and practical work. The former involved the public and politicians, the latter what they hoped to accomplish at Mesa Verde. Those included an initial survey of the ruins and the land. They already organized plans for, or had crews constructing, wagon roads and trails, digging water wells, working on restoration of partially caved in buildings and towers, excavating for relics, building stairways to otherwise inaccessible ruins and erecting a hotel. The women brought leading scholars and archaeologists to the sites to try to gain their support.

They would not accomplish all their goals. Undaunted, the women worked on the political front, convincing Congress and the president to create a national park. With the federal government behind them, they believed they could push ahead with all their plans.

Park bill after park bill withered and died in committees as Washington seemed reluctant to take that step. The women pressed ahead, redoubling their lobbying efforts. Various opponents held them up, from those concerned about what this precedent might mean in the future, to groups arguing over who would have the right to excavate the ruins. Some people were even concerned about a novel idea, what would happen to the Utes? Much of the proposed park land was within their reservation. Also, a few people had homesteaded within the planned boundaries and they appeared none too happy with the park plan.

Unfortunately, unanimity did not reside within the movement either. McClurg had only been reluctantly converted to the national park idea. She long favored a park controlled by Colorado, and/or women, primarily because she felt she would have more say in its operation. Finally in 1906, everything came together. The education, promotion, and lobbying at last paid off, although it also helped to have Theodore Roosevelt in the White House with his interest in the West, history, and conservation. Various other groups, such as the Nebraska Academy of Sciences and the Colorado State Forestry Association, provided added support.

Proponents called attention to the national significance of the ruins, the vandalism that already had occurred, the unsuitability of the land for agricultural purposes, and the potential tourist market. The House and Senate finally both approved the Mesa Verde National Park bill, and President Roosevelt signed it on June 29.

Sadly, just before their moment of triumph the women's movement fell apart, the victim of differing philosophies, strong personalities, and urban jealousies. Peabody had always supported the national park idea, which McClurg only did reluctantly. Each had her own ardent supporters and reasons. Worried about the Secretary of Interior being given control, McClurg favored the Association being in charge. Therefore the state park plan seemed best. Reluctantly, she backed off that idea, only to reverse her position in 1906 and revert to favoring state control. Meanwhile, she also considered the idea of having her husband become the superintendent, a tactic that obviously would have given her continuing influence in the park. In her mind, Mesa Verde almost become "her park."

The women made an attempt to keep their dispute quiet and out of the press, but failed. Both factions jumped in, issuing statements, attacking and denying, while the public witnessed a dismaying dissolution of unity. One association member quaintly observed, it all "precipitated a warm fight."

Denver supported Peabody, while Colorado Springs, and somewhat reluctantly Pueblo, rallied behind McClurg. The *Denver Post* (February 26, 1906) said, "In fifty years from now if the government of the United States takes care of those Cliff Dwellings, the whole world will know of them." In the end, Peabody resigned from the Association, losing the battle, but winning the war. The fight did not end in 1906, but carried on for more than another generation, dimming the contributions of the women toward saving and creating the park. In a pique, McClurg went off and helped create her own "cliff dwelling" at Manitou Springs.

The women had saved Mesa Verde and the fight to get it created as a national park. Along the way, they had helped build the first wagon road into the mesa, appropriated $1,000 for a survey, developed a spring at Spruce Tree House, produced the first accurate map of the area, and arranged for archaeologists to visit the ruins. They encouraged scholars and scientists to do more than come to Mesa Verde. The women wanted them to examine, dig, and study. Equally as important, and in some ways more so, they had distributed photographs, books and pamphlets, sponsored relic displays, and probably given more than 100 talks and lectures on the cliff dwellings to awaken public interest. Their lobbying and persistence directly influenced Congress in creating the national park. Despite the split in their ranks, they would continue to be active at the park for another decade, including helping financially to restore Balcony House.

First and foremost stood their accomplishment in creating Mesa Verde National Park, the first archaeological national park in the world. Preservation caught on and other sites soon followed, including Chaco Canyon, Aztec Ruins, Hovenweep, and Bandelier. All initially became national monuments and some eventually evolved into national parks.

At the same time as the creation of Mesa Verde, Congress passed the Antiquities Act that worked toward protecting and preserving the nation's prehistoric and historic archaeological resources and sites. The government also wanted to improve the availability of such sites to the public, a must if such places were to be set aside. A cost-conscious Congress and public, meanwhile, needed to be convinced that such developments benefited the largest number of people.

Another hope, expressed by writer Eugene Parsons in a 1906 article, looked to public awareness.

> Hitherto Westerners have been too busy making a living and getting rich to bother their heads much about cliff dwellings and cave homes, but the time will come when men and women will feel a curiosity to know something of the prehistoric past of the Southwest.

His prediction proved absolutely correct.

Some of those same westerners looked about and saw an economic windfall sitting on their doorsteps. They already had an interest in those prehistoric ruins and people, a monetary interest in dollars and cents. Now visions of potentially more profit danced before them. All this would come with increased tourism. Some worried that the park might limit another profitable activity, the collecting and selling of relics to those same visitors. Others fretted about locking up natural resources within parks from public development.

The future would be fascinating and challenging. Visitors were coming, and they did not worry about such matters. Westerners were waiting for them and the money they carried in their wallets and purses.

SOURCES

Books
Crofutt, George, *Crofutt's Grip-Sack Guide of Colorado* (Omaha: Overland Publishing, 1885): 163.

Smith, Duane A., M*esa Verde National Park* (Boulder: University Press of Colorado, 2002 revised edition), chapters 3 and 4.

A Week at the Fair (Chicago: Rand, McNally & Company, 1893): 102, 235, & 246.

Smith, Duane A., *Women to the Rescue, Creating Mesa Verde National Park* (Durango: Durango Herald Small Press, 2005)

Articles
Birdsall, William R., "The Cliff Dwellings of the Canons of the Mesa Verde," *American Geographical Society Bulletin* (December 31, 1891): 585-87.

Chapin, Frederick H., "Cliff Dwellings of the Mancos Canons," *The American Antiquarian* (July 1890): 195-96

Eldredge, Effie, quoted in "Packing into Mesa Verde - 1903 Style," *Four Corners Magazine* (summer 1972): 60-61.

Fossett, Frank, Colorado (Denver: *Daily Tribune*, 1876): 437.

Gannett, Henry, "Prehistoric Ruins in Southern Colorado," *Popular Science Review* (1880): 666-67.

Hardacre, Emma C., "The Cliff-Dwellers," *Scribner's Monthly* (December, 1878): 266-69.

Henderson, Alice, "The Cliff-Dwellers," *The Independent*, June 22, 1893.

Henderson, Palmer, "The Cliff Dwellers," *The Literary Northwest* (May 1893): 79.

Jackson, William H., "Report," *Annual Report of the United States Geological and Geographical Survey* (Washington: Government Printing Office, 1876): 370.

McClurg, Gilbert & Virginia, "The Development of the Mesa Verde National Park," *Travel* (July 1916): 36.

Morgan, Wm. Fellowes, "Description of a Cliff-House on the Mancos River ...," *American Association for the Advancement of Science Proceedings* (1879): 300.

Newell, F. H., "Mesa Verde," *National Geographic* (October 1898): 431-33, 434.

Parsons, Eugene, "The Mesa Verde National Park," *The American Antiquarian* (1906): 266.

Publications
Denver Republican, October 13, 1898.
Denver Times, June 29, 1915.
Mancos Times, October 13, 1899; October 20, 1899.
Rocky Mountain News, March 5, 1876; October 29, 1899.

Correspondence
Fred Cowling to Frank McNitt, no date, Wetherill Collection, Mesa Verde National Park.

2

Three Little Towns and Tourism

By Duane A. Smith

E ven before the birth of Mesa Verde National Park, tourists had come. They brought with them dollars, money that economically stressed southwestern Coloradans sorely needed. These local folks, and many western contemporaries, ardently believed in the words written long ago in Ecclesiastes, "A feast is made for laughter, and wine market merry: but money answereth all things."

For an isolated area barely out of its frontier days, with an as yet poorly defined economic base, this bonanza promised a fresh start with a pocketful of new possibilities. For struggling nearby communities, tourism aroused the desire to dominate the traveling public's destination and spending, even if it meant leaving no stone unturned to undermine a neighbor. Such urban rivalries were nothing if not no-holds-barred! In a victor-takes-all struggle, the spoils were enticing. As the communities prospered, their counties' rural population would enjoy better times, or so they assumed. For Colorado and its three neighboring territories, the park and increased tourism offered opportunities for promotion and growth. If visitors came, some might stay, or tell others. In a "grow or die" world, that hit the heart of tomorrow. Many assumptions and hopes underlay these expectations, usual themes in Western history.

Animas Museum Photo Archive

John Moss

So Mesa Verde arrived into the world already sparking high expectations among neighbors and sure to create jealousies. Around it sat two little villages and one town which proudly proclaimed itself a city. By 1906, each of the three – Mancos, Durango, and Cortez in order of their founding – had laid claim to the title of Mesa Verde's "gateway." Their aspirations appeared similar, the economic bases of the two were similar, but their potential and development would prove quite dissimilar. Undaunted, residents believed that hard work, promotion, growth, and numerous investors would overcome all doubters. Forget reality, grasp hope and ignore Ben Franklin's admonition, "he that lives upon hope will die fasting." Numerous little crossroads hamlets and more distant towns played only a minor role in what would develop through the coming decades.

Mancos, the oldest of the three and highest in elevation, lacked no confidence. Mining man, promoter, and entrepreneur John Moss, who had opened mines in La Plata Canyon and started the fledgling camp of Parrott

City, established a ranch in the valley in the early 1870s. Others followed his lead and in response to their needs, the little village of Mancos grew. Development came very slowly in the next decade and not until 1890 would the Mancos precinct appear in the census report. While the precinct counted 635 people that year, it would have to wait to 1900 before the census takers made a separate tally for the town, 383.

The fertile valley had "stock and agricultural advantages," and already had gained notoriety for the nearby "ancient ruins of towns and cities, built by an extinct race of people." It gained a post office, even if misspelled initially as Mancas, and according to Fossett, in his 1880 *Colorado*, had 17 farms with 2,720 acres under cultivation.

Out-of-the-way and small, Mancos quickly found itself overshadowed by its rival neighbor Durango as it swiftly gained an all-important railroad connection. Mancos yearned for one, but had to wait impatiently for another decade before the rails arrived. George Crofutt's *Grip-Sack Guide to Colorado* (1885) could only characterize Mancos as "...a small agricultural town where grain, except corn, and all kinds of vegetables grow to perfection. Stock-raising is also an important industry." Small! That hurt boosters' pride and visions. Its only claim to fame was "along the river are many old ruins of cliff houses." Frederick Chapin offered a more favorable image a few years later. "Mancos is an inviting place for its own sake, as well as for its being a point of departure for the archaeological wonders of the neighboring canons."

The Wetherills' Alamo Ranch also impressed him. "Everything about the Alamo Ranch gives evidence of thrift and comfort. The barns are large and well filled, and enormous stacks of hay and straw are near the corral. The whole neighboring scene is pastoral: a picturesque home has been established in the wilderness of sage-brush and pinon-pine." It, Chapin stressed, offered a place "at which to stop and rest" on the trip to Mesa Verde.

Mancos had one advantage it never failed to mention and herald, the Wetherills called it home. The *Mancos Times* praised the family (they were what "energy and perseverance will accomplish in the west"), and the ranch as the "mecca" for tourists. The Wetherills charged $2 per day for board and lodging at the ranch with its "first class" accommodations. To go into the ruins they were "amply prepared to provide" guides, horses, camp equipment, and supplies all for $5 per person. "Tourists unaccustomed to such mode of living need have no fear of danger or discomfort." Sadly for Mancos, however, the Wetherills lost their ranch because of poor management. By 1902, they all had left the valley.

Durango, that product of the Animas City Council's miscalculation, grew the fastest. From no residents in September 1880, it multiplied to around 2,000 – some claimed more – come Christmas time that year. By the next May, it was incorporated and the city fathers sallied forth to make

Mesa Verde National Park

Alamo Ranch, with Point Lookout in the distance.

it a town settlers, investors, and visitors would love to come to and, most momentously, to stay. A Denver & Rio Grande town, the "Denver of the Southwest," the "bound to boom" town, Durango promptly raced past rival Animas City, which never recovered. Within a year, the "wonder of the southwest" grabbed the county seat designation from the tiny mining camp of Parrott City nestled at the mouth of La Plata Canyon. Too far away, Durangoans thought, spelling the end of any importance for that community.

Urban rivalries and fights left many communities defeated and their hopes crushed. Durango held several advantages and parlayed them with a sure hand. It gained the railroad, the 19th century's transportation sensation, before any of its rivals. Not only that, several of D&RG's movers and shakers became Durango's movers and shakers with finances, connections, and abilities. They started the smelter, which eventually developed into a regional smelter working ore from throughout the San Juans. Feisty newspapers leaped onto the scene to promote, defend, agitate, bulldog rivals, and dream the dreams of wonderful tomorrows. They also came up with slogans for the "magic city on the banks of the Animas." With four news-

Amon Carter Museum

1890s Durango became the railroad and tourist hub for Mesa Verde.

papers in its first year, Durango had plenty of bombast and rebuttals to hurl at pesky, upstart rivals. No nearby rival came close to matching that onslaught.

It was located in the valley of the Animas River, with a steady water supply and a hundred-day growing season. Ranchers and farmers proliferated in all directions around it, hemmed in only by the Southern Ute reservation two miles south. The proximity of the reservation worried some people, but Durango offered an answer – move the Utes. Uncle Sam eased worries and helped Durango along the way by building Fort Lewis 14 miles to the southwest. Those government contracts and jobs, along with the security of knowing troops were available if needed, provided further support in Durango's first decade. The existence of coal almost in town – one reason D&RG had been interested in the location to begin with – and a forest nearby for lumber helped balance the town's economy. Gaining the La Plata County seat gave the "metropolis" additional political power.

A beautiful mountainous location, railroad connections with Denver and elsewhere, and such attractions as the Utes and mountain mining camps (often considered "wild and wicked") for trade and tourism, and the ruins of the "ancients" gave it a start the town never relinquished. Those 19th-century medical cure-alls – the nearby hot springs – and a salubrious climate (Durangoans claimed it to be exceedingly healthful) brought in tourists, health seekers, and adventurers. Investors saw bountiful possibilities.

Colorado Historical Society

Cortez, around 1910, lagged behind its rivals.

That was Durango by the time the Wetherills brought their first collection of relics into town and soon found they could charge admission. Because of an early hesitancy to appreciate what lay at their doorstep, Durangoans did not buy the Wetherills' collection when they had the chance. Making up for a lost opportunity, they soon grasped the potential and moved swiftly to dominate the game.

Cortez arrived on the scene the last of the three gateway rival communities. It started last and stayed last for over half a century. No railroad gave it birth. Like most of its farming contemporaries, it just appeared and grew very slowly. A few settlers moved into the neighborhood in the mid-1880s, joining the cattlemen already there. Just as Mancos had drawn the Wetherills, the milder climate and winter grazing lured ranchers. At the time, though, they all were part of La Plata County, making them subservient to the county seat whose political power, transportation hub, and business heart sat 50 miles away in Durango.

Cortez came into existence in December 1886, but would not even be incorporated for years. The little farming and ranching settlement grew sluggishly as Lee Kelly, who arrived there years later by stage, indicated. He remembered it consisted of one restaurant, two livery stables, a blacksmith shop and saloon. The crew building the water ditches camped on Main Street and spent their evenings shooting prairie dogs from their tent fronts. Cortez slowly gained the trappings of civilization – school, homes, businesses, church, brass band, and a newspaper, the *Montezuma Journal* (that Kelly somehow overlooked) which declared to its readers on April 28, 1888, "We hope to give to the people of the Montezuma Valley a paper that shall worthy champion their interests and be effective in promoting the same."

Veteran Colorado editor John Curry did his best, but unlike his counterparts in Durango he faced serious obstacles. The valley and town remained so short of water that the Colorado Consolidated Land and Water Company tried to solve the problem with a tunnel bringing water in from the Dolores River through canals. On September 7, 1897, however, the *Journal* recommended to its readers that "proper diligence" would allow them to avoid the usual winter problem of running out of good water, and being "compelled to use very bad water."

They would resolve that problem eventually, but they never overcame another. The railroad, despite local hopes, never chugged into Cortez. Dolores offered the nearest station, 12 miles away. The *Journal* (April 7, 1899) never gave up hope, as the editor dreamed of "a railroad through the valley with an outlet to the coast, then the coal mines will be opened, and this section will resemble a mighty arsenal of industry, and the valley blossom as a garden." It would never occur. Even worse, those coal deposits unfortunately happened to fall within the park boundaries.

Cortez did gain one thing that boded well for its future. The Legislature created Montezuma County out of the western part of La Plata County in 1889 with Cortez designated as the county seat. Although some La Plata County residents grumbled and did not appreciate losing the western portion of their county, the *Herald* did not stand among them. Its April 16, 1889, issue wished its new neighbor well and predicted that Montezuma's coal and agricultural resources would soon rank it with "any county" in the state. Potential it had, but isolated in far southwestern Colorado, Cortez would have to live on hope for several generations before it blossomed.

The other component in the developing story of tourism and transportation was the Rio Grande Southern Railroad. Veteran Colorado railroad and mining man Otto Mears wanted to tap the mines at Rico, Ophir, and Telluride which had no railroad connections. Furthermore, he had been frustrated by the impossibly steep grade down the Uncompahgre Canyon from the Red Mountain mining district to Ouray. As a result, he decided to build a railroad around the western side of the San Juan Mountains and over Lizard Head Pass to reach and connect these various districts.

Incorporated in November 1889, the line was surveyed the next year, and grading started. Construction crews worked from both ends, Durango and Ridgway, where the Rio Grande Southern connected into the Denver & Rio Grande system. The railroad tied the two segments together on December 19, 1891, with the first through train on January 2, 1892.

While there remained a great deal of work to be done to make it profitable, Mears had completed his dream.

The 172-mile route accessed coal fields, gold and silver mines, farms, ranches, and communities. It also carried tourists to the mountains, mining camps, and Mesa Verde. The Rio Grande Southern reached Mancos, 38 miles from Durango, in April 1891. A planned line to Cortez never materialized and most of the traveling public never reached Cortez. Unfortunately for Mears, his dreams of profits quickly fell by the wayside. The crash and depression of 1893, the worst America had yet endured, along with the collapse of the price of silver which staggered San Juan mining, placed the railroad in receivership. It had barely been operating a year and a half when disaster hit. Mears lost his little line, and it fell under the control of the Denver & Rio Grande, which had owned large amounts of Rio Grande Southern bonds from the start.

The line continued operating under its original name, yet never achieved its promise. While tourism now assumed a more important role, it could never replace the expected mining revenues. Nevertheless, the Rio Grande Southern and the D&RG promoted tourism. The far-famed "Circle Tour" took visitors from Denver to Durango or Ridgway over the Denver & Rio Grande. Here a decision needed to be made to go over the Rio Grande Southern, or go on to Ouray, up the Uncompahgre Canyon by stage, then from Ironton to Silverton to Durango by rail. Or, if arriving in Durango from Denver, the traveler had to make the decision in the opposite direction. The spectacular scenery, hot springs, and mining towns provided obvious attractions. So did those ruins near Mancos. The railroad enthusiastically promoted this idea in its advertisements. "This line brings the tourist within easy ride of the wonderful HOMES of the CLIFF DWELLERS." With the Denver and Rio Grande, the Rio Grande Southern formed the "unsurpassed" all-rail "Around the Circle Trip." To entice tourists even more, they also called the route the "Rainbow Route."

The Denver & Rio Grande promoted Mesa Verde extensively, an obvious profitable venture for it. In May 1893, a special car arrived at Mancos bringing, among others, newspaper editors, prominent easterners, and William Henry Jackson, who once again took photographs. The *Mancos Times* (May 26) proudly announced that the visitors, gratified with their trip, would be "always ready to put in a good word for Mancos in the future." Appreciating such free publicity, the *Times* (August 13, 1897) also complimented the railroad for its new "Tourists' Guide to the Cliff Dwelling Ruins," an "ornament to any library" that dealt "solely" with the cliff dwellings and how to reach them.

The railroad told readers that Wetherill & Sons would make prompt replies to any inquiry and "gladly make necessary arrangements." The D&RG, as well, would be glad to furnish information and, as might be imagined, the "Guide" praised the other attractions along the two lines.

Sometimes, though, at least in the eyes of Mancos, the railroad did not play fair. Conductors were prohibited from issuing "stop-over, or lay-over tickets," which riled the *Times* (September 11, 1896). They should issue them to "those who desire to visit the Cliff Dwellings and other points of interest off the railroad." That would, the paper concluded, "greatly increase" the Mancos tourist travel. The railroad might be promoting Mesa Verde, but it was nonetheless determined to make extra money from people who wanted to stop in Mancos to visit there.

The next year the Denver & Rio Grande did reduce the ticket price from Durango to Mancos to $4, putting them on sale from May to October and honoring them for 60 days. The railroad stressed that the tourists' headquarters could be either in Durango with its "1st class hotel accommodations," or in Mancos at the Alamo Ranch. Mancos did not like the fact that Durango received better publicity because the $4 rate was "convenient and cheap for those who desire to establish permanent headquarters in Durango where the advantage of metropolitan hotels would be found."

Local folks appreciated that the Rio Grande Southern publicized "the Wonderful Homes of the Cliff Dwellers" near Mancos. Even Durango saw a blessing in this, despite the fact it seemed to help Mancos the most, because the railroad brought, said the July 15, 1892, *Herald*, the "tourist, within easy ride" of the ruins. Get them to Durango and "certainly" they would be attracted to stay and see the other sights while enjoying the community's refinements.

Mancos suffered because its desired railroad connection ran through arch-rival Durango. Nonetheless, the small town could and did eagerly advertise itself as the home of the Wetherills, and as the "gateway" to Mesa Verde. That only elevated an already simmering rivalry and jealousy between the two communities.

Their newspapers loyally championed the virtues of their home communities, while at the same time righteously attacking their rival, or at least pointing out its "backwardness." Like kittens and puppies, they hissed and barked, scratched and bit. Behind it all lurked a deadly seriousness. No guarantee existed in the West that a young community would survive. So they strove to gain every advantage possible. Durango's early newspapers and railroad connections started it off strongly, but Mancos finally gained the Rio Grande Southern and its own paper. Now both could compete for Mesa Verde tourists on a more level plain, if not with equal resources.

Mancos lit into Durango's pretensions right from the start. The *Times* emerged especially confident after gold was discovered on the west slope of the La Plata Mountains. Crowed the paper on May 12, 1893, "Mancos will contain a population of 3,000 before 60 days roll around." Then the editor continued on: "Durango will awake to the fact that within 60 days

A view of Mancos, looking toward Mesa Verde. Mesa Verde National Park

her streets will be deserted and many business houses will close." Not content with this bombast, the article concluded, "Mancos will never rival her. She will outstrip her as badly as our foot-racer did last Sunday." Foot racing (sprints) and baseball teams defended a town's honor as well as collecting bets on the side for lucky boosters.

The *Times* did not stop. In the August 18 issue it concluded that every "resident on this side of the La Platas" had not long ago "made up his or her mind that it is simply useless to expect even common, every-day courtesy, much less any kind of assistance or encouragement from the hands or utterances of people or the press of Durango." Apparently, they had stung them a bit and seeing why was easy. According to the paper when strangers made inquiries in Durango about Mancos, they were "given to understand it was the rendezvous of cattle and horse thieves, desperados and murderers." As a result, "not one single citizen has a good or kind word to say of their neighbor denizens of the 'smelter city' as they are pleased to term their five-cent-beer burg."

Apparently, the accusation had a basis in reality. Well-known mountaineer and writer Frederick Chapin arrived in 1889 to see the newly discovered sites. He naturally came to Durango, "the principal town [that idea galled Mancos no end] in southwest Colorado." Then Chapin encountered a challenge. "It seemed difficult to obtain much information in regard to the now not far distant Mancos country." In fact, he concluded, if he had not been well-informed, his party "should have been led to turn aside to visit the ruins of minor importance that exist in the lower valley of the Animas and which have already been fully described – this upon the representation of enthusiastic residents of that valley." Chapin judged that, "it was but by the merest accident that we found ourselves instead at the delightful ranch of the Wetherills, on the banks of the Mancos."

Nor did it stop when the century turned. The June 14, 1901, *Times* included this blast about misinformation Durangoans gave visitors, "They were informed that they could drive from Durango to Cliff Palace in carriages, thus avoiding the tedious horse-back ride from Mancos." The editor decided, "these things are laughable, but extremely annoying."

Part of the problem derived from the fact that Durango, since its inception, had considered itself the region's crown jewel and all-important "metropolis." An 1883 pamphlet, for example, explained why. "Rome was built upon seven hills. Durango's future is built upon seven agricultural valleys…" Those seven included the Mancos Valley, much to the disgust, if not resentment, of its residents. Durango also, the paper boasted, had coal, lumber, accessibility, hot springs for the invalid, an altitude best for agriculture, and nearby mining town and mines.

Durango showed more restraint than did Mancos, reflecting, no doubt, its stronger position. The depression of the 1890s hurt everyone and intensified the need to promote. Durango had a Board of Trade whose object was "to advertise the city and promote its interests." It did and so did local newspapers, praising new hotels, such as the Strater, coining creative slogans "Gateway of the San Juan Country," and feverishly championing everything about Durango. "There is no place like Colorado and Durango is the gem of the state." "Clean, bright, beautiful, and healthful" Durango beckoned, a place no tourist would want to miss.

The *Mancos Times* and local Mancos businesses tried as hard as they could. The *Times* even included a drawing of a cliff dwelling on its masthead which should have convinced all but a dullard that Mancos provided the place for a grand adventure into Mesa Verde. The Hotel Lemmon, for example, jumped into the fray as well – the "only first class hotel in the valley," – and it provided free buses to and from all trains. Not stopping there, the management promised, "Tourists to the Mancos Cliff Dwellings and gold mines" would be provided with guides, animals, bedding, and camp "equipage."

The *Mancos Times* never missed a beat promoting the community as a tourist Mecca. It listed "new arrivals" (guests at the Alamo Ranch), "tourists coming," "guides and outfitters ready for all who may come," and praised the "beautiful" Mancos valley.

Of the three communities, Mancos most quickly appreciated what Mesa Verde might mean. The one and only thing that would make it stand out among the other western communities trying to attract visitors was the Cliff Dweller ruins. Other towns had beautiful valleys, first-class hotels, and everything, but none sat next to anything like Mesa Verde. Mancos would not brook any competition, yet two challengers crowded in also trying to seize the opportunity. Cortez fell under its attack first.

The reason Mancos turned its attention to Cortez was not only that it sneakily tried to cut into Mancos's tourist trade. More significantly, Cortez appeared to have a weaker base, and thus was easier to knock out. It struggled under noticeable handicaps, including no railroad connection or decent roads to the west, north, and south. Undaunted, Cortez pressed ahead. With a small population, infant agricultural hinterland, no mineral resources, and a tiny business district, Cortez held no cards.

Mancos's animosity did not deter locals or the *Montezuma Journal*. It proclaimed on June 2, 1899 that the cliff dwellings "will be the center attraction for a large number of tourists this season." The next weekly issue declared that the finest "preserved" cliff dwellings could be reached more easily from Cortez. The distance was only 15 miles with good water "over the best, nearest, and most picturesque routes." The way to reach them "is via the Rio Grande Southern Railroad to Dolores." From there, connections could be made by stage to Cortez. That aggravated Mancos no end, since such travelers had to pass right through their town.

In Cortez, Sterl Thomas advertised that he could "fit you out with guides, saddle, tents, rigs, [and] pack horses." Interpreters could also be found "who speak all the tongues of the west – Ute, Navajo, Spanish and Greaser." Not to mention that Thomas could "read the hieroglyphics of the builders of those ruins!" Such amazing statements often appeared in the struggle to gain any type of advantage. Thomas also offered "just grand" photograph views ("some of the finest") of Cliff Palace, Spruce Tree House, and other ruins.

Mancos begged to disagree. "The *Montezuma Journal* editor should get a sectional map of the country before making the broad assertion that Cortez is 12 miles nearer the Cliff Dwellings than is Mancos. Facts will not bear him out in any such rot." Continuing, the editor finished with a jab, "the fact is, it is more difficult to get from the foot of the trail on the Cortez side, to Spruce Tree House, than it [is] the entire ride from Mancos."

The paper pointed out with glee that the Cortez guides refused to show their more reasonable trail. In 1901, Mancos went after Cortez because its guides "get lost about every time" they try to make a trip to the ruins, or so it claimed. Cortez tried to "make the suckers believe it is closer to Cliff Palace against all reason and sense."

Twelve-year-old Minnie Hickman rode into Mesa Verde over Cortez's trail in 1904. She concurred with Mancos. It was not "much of a trail." Her horse had to leap over a log to keep on the trail in one place. Despite that, she "enjoyed" the trip. By then, Cortez had dropped to last among the competing communities and would remain there for half a century. Apparently realizing this fact, the *Journal* decreased its coverage of Mesa Verde and even came close to ignoring the creation of the national park completely.

Still, other problems persisted for Mancos, one being the lack of an adequate road. Getting into Mesa Verde required traveling over trails that at best could be rough and steep. The Rio Grande Southern decided to help visitors by constructing a toll road. They planned to have it open by the summer of 1900 when a hotel would also be ready for patrons. The railroad planned to donate the initial $100 to the road fund "if citizens of Mancos would donate a like amount." That amount, the Wetherill brothers assured them, would "be sufficient to build a very good wagon road" to intersect the "easy trails" to the different ruins.

The *Times* supported the idea and urged hotel- and liverymen to take the initiative. Nothing came of either project. The women's group planned a public "highway" asserting they could "save money by building the road down the Rio Mancos." That also died aborning.

One solution to road access problems would be creation of a park, which Mancos wholeheartedly supported. It appeared to them that people in Durango, and perhaps Cortez, were working against them and the Cliff Dwellings Association by opposing the women in their attempt to lease the land from the Ute Mountain Utes. The *Times* also could not believe "knockers" would obstruct the women in their road building project.

Durango and Mancos newspapers followed, with interest, the vicissitudes of the park bills in those early years of the 1900s. Despite their local differences, both towns wanted the park to quickly become a reality. Visits by noted scientists, influential women, plus eastern correspondents created excitement in the communities. Such parties, they assumed hopefully, would "advertise the ruins more extensively than ever ... before" and would induce "hundreds of tourists" to come.

Whether or not the attention brought "hundreds" of tourists, one tour did generate a feature story in the *New York Herald*, a positive step forward. Meanwhile, infighting among the women garnered more attention in Denver, Colorado Springs, and Pueblo, where most of them lived, than it did in Mancos and Durango.

By April 1906, victory apparently drew near.

The *Mancos Times-Tribune* (the two local papers had merged) in May foresaw only blessings ahead. As surveyors under the direction of the Secretary of the Interior, finished their work, the editor exulted that it appeared the creation of a national park would happen "in only a matter of a comparatively short time." What effect would that have locally? "This means that the government is going to spend thousands of dollars building roadways, making the park easy access for visitors, cleaning and beautifying the park, constructing hotels and drilling artesian wells."

For the cash-hungry region, that meant jobs, contracts, supplies sales, potential growth, and publicity. "The making of all these improvements will necessitate the expenditure of a considerable sum of money for this part of the county."

The newspaper just knew a cornucopia of blessings would shower over Mancos and its neighborhood. The paramount development would be a first-class hotel to handle the tourist trade. Then "fishing, hunting, boating and other pleasurable amusements" on nearby lakes would follow and possibly a health sanitarium would be built. Fruit and truck farming "will add not a little to farmer and gardener" activities. All this aside "the benefits derived from publicity" would be immeasurable. The result of such developments would be the "important and far-reaching up building of this country."

"UNCLE SAM HAD AIDED WITH THE CREATION OF TOWNS, REGIONAL PROMOTION, AND THE COMING OF THE RAILROAD AS WELL ... "

Such enthusiasm remained high. By June, the *Times-Tribune* envisioned Mancos becoming a first-class town. The editor had conveniently forgotten the bust of the gold excitement, the earlier hope to become "first class." The La Plata Mountains disappointed many in these years when gold teased but did not satisfy the community's or investors' hopes. Not to fret, the past did not worry locals. Mancos had all the other resources to gain that stature – "fertile lands, first class water and lots of it, good timber, coal, gold [they never gave up hope!], stone, and splendid scenery and climate." The editor warned, however, "let us remember that cities are made not grown, and the making depends upon the citizens themselves."

That concisely and expectantly summarized what southwestern Coloradans believed – perhaps dreamed would be a better word – would come to them through Mesa Verde National Park. They had long relied on Washington to help them out and settle this region with the Homestead Act, the establishment of post offices, generous mining and timber claims, Indian policy, and finally the building of Fort Lewis and stationing of troops there for a decade. Uncle Sam had aided with the creation of towns, regional promotion, and the coming of the railroad as well, although William J. Palmer did not take land grants for his D&RG.

The West might seem like a place for rugged individualists to independently carve out their futures, fame, and fortunes, but they had a partner upon whom they repeatedly relied, their Uncle Sam. Their Uncle had been a generous benefactor.

When news arrived of President Roosevelt signing the park bill, the

Mancos newspaper headline said it all. "Mancos is IT. Mesa Verde National Park." Crusty old Dave Day expressed nothing in his *Durango Democrat*, but he understood what the park meant. Back on April 13, he too had predicted the park's creation would mean that the government would spend thousands of dollars on such things as roads, trails, artesian wells, and such buildings as would be necessary. The *Durango Herald* and the *Montezuma Journal* remained strangely silent in June and July. Other state and national events caught their attention.

Maybe their silence reflected jealousy. Mancos had gained the first plum by being named the park headquarters. That further strengthened its hand on gathering visitors and dollars.

Durangoans' newspapers might have taken the official park creation with a blasé attitude, but many of their readers looked forward to the day when tourists would make their town "it," as Mancos expressed it. Almost from Durango's beginning, tourists had been coming and now another attraction sat virtually at their doorstep, or so they liked to believe.

Tourists had come, but Mancos had gotten the better of it. The Wetherills' registration book at the Alamo Ranch totaled nearly 1,000 names during 1889-1901, which provides the best indication available of how many travelers came to see the ruins. Obviously, others visited the ruins using different guides or simply wandering about on their own. The first full year of the park's operation, 1907, 73 visitors were recorded. That figure must be considered the first reliable count and is not greatly different from the yearly average that the Wetherills recorded.

Sometimes the visitors did not enjoy their visit as much as locals would have liked. Mancos Valley resident Ina Allein recounted a story which raised questions about guides' reliability. "My mother told me of the experience of a young 'dude' whom they'd [Wetherills] taken up to the ruins, but he got lost & after two days came to my grandfather's ranch (4 miles from Mancos) thirsty & hungry. They had to carry him inside to take care of him, but it was said the Wetherills made little effort to find him."

Obviously, Mesa Verde had not yet become a major tourist attraction or made a major impact on the local economy. Undaunted, these southwestern Coloradans looked to its potential for salvation. Potential it had, because Yellowstone National Park, the first national park, had also started small then grown steadily. The present remained promising though and considering the isolation and economic trials of the Mancos Valley and, to a lesser degree Durango, any financial help was most welcome.

As 1906 ended, Mesa Verde National Park closed for the season. It had finished the year staffed with local political appointees, another somewhat unexpected blessing. Experience had been gained in park operations and everyone looked forward to the new year.

Acting superintendent William Leonard made a report of his October visit to the park. Despite "two whole days of this trip" made in a snowstorm, he gathered the information needed. His recommendations spoke to the present and future. In his opinion, Mancos on the Rio Grande Southern Railroad "is the nearest and most accessible point for the public to outfit for the park." However, roads into the park and to ruins within it needed work. Washington's action on these recommendations would place Mancos in the driver's seat for the next 16 years.

For the time being, Cortez was out of the "gateway" competition. Mancos had crowned itself with that appellation with a certain amount of justification beyond local back-patting. No community lay closer to the park, had been involved with Mesa Verde from the start of the Wetherills' discovery, or had better guides for leading trips in to the ruins. Durango, nonetheless, lurked in the near background coveting the gateway crown and scheming to capture it.

Transportation achieved its 19th century zenith now that the Denver & Rio Grande and the Rio Grande Southern railroads reached Durango and Mancos. The railroad ride provided speed, comfort, and convenience especially when considering what travel had been before 1881 and 1891 when the two rail lines were completed. The scenery seemingly improved too, when viewed from the comfort of a passenger or parlor car. Not all concerns were resolved, however. Isolation remained a problem, despite the railroad cutting the trip from Denver from weeks to days. Mesa Verde remained a long way from American population centers. In spite of the arrival of the iron horse, the park still sat well off the beaten path for tourists.

To the west, north, and south, transportation had not improved all that much. The nearest railroad stations were located at Albuquerque and Gallup, New Mexico. Roads from there to Mesa Verde did not lend themselves to comfortable or rapid travel. Nor had the roads within the park noticeably improved in the past years. As Superintendent William Leonard pointed out, it still took a day's ride from Mancos. Carriage and wagon travel awaited better roads.

With Mesa Verde achieving national park status, promotion of the region and state gained an invaluable agent. Railroads, towns, counties, state, and federal government would join toward the goal of making Mesa Verde a traveler's destination. It might take a while, as it had in Yellowstone National Park. Still, Yellowstone had overcome, within a reasonable time, some of the same problems now faced at Mesa Verde – isolation, difficult connections with the outside world, lack of accommodations, and poor roads within the park. Not only had it overcome them, Yellowstone had emerged as a tourist destination and a recognized national treasure that already was attracting international attention and visitors. Optimistically, Mesa Verde proponents hoped for no less in its future.

In the excitement of the park's creation, one fact probably garnered little attention. Control of Mesa Verde National Park remained totally in the hands of Washington and the Department of the Interior. Virginia

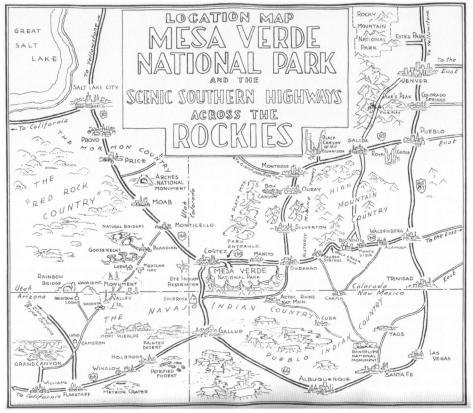

Mesa Verde Company/Mesa Verde National Park

**A map that was featured in a booklet published in 1954.
The booklet promoting Mesa Verde, and titled such, was authored by Ansel F. Hall.**

McClurg had worried about that issue, primarily for personal motives like wanting her husband to be superintendent and retaining her influence at Mesa Verde. Others of her followers wholeheartedly backed federal control. That had been one major issue that caused the breakup of the women's movement. What federal control might mean for local people and their communities would be decided another day. Some people had an idea. They already did not like the creation of national forests, not only in Colorado, but throughout the West. Rural westerners especially did not appreciate President Roosevelt and his enthusiasm for the conservation movement. Suddenly some of their perceived rights, such as development of natural resources, timber harvesting, and livestock grazing, had been taken away.

As 1907 dawned, an expectation floated in the air of what would be coming in a very short time, or so the boosters supposed. Problems needed to be resolved by the park's superintendent, federal government, and the local communities. Tomorrow rested in their hands.

SOURCES

Books
Chapin, Frederick, *The Land of the Cliff-Dwellers* (Boston: W. B. Clarke, 1892): 99-101.
Crofutt, George, *Crofutt's Grip-Sack Guide of Colorado* (Omaha: Overland Publishing, 1885)
Ferrell, Mallory Hope, *Silver San Juan: The Rio Grande Southern Railroad* (Boulder: Pruett Publishing, 1973): 47-55, & 82.
Fletcher, Maurine S. (ed.), *The Wetherills of the Mesa Verde* (Rutherford: Associated University Presses, 1977): 181
Fossett, Frank, *Colorado* (New York: C. G. Crawford, 1880): 192, 194, & 356-57.

Publications
Durango Evening Herald, April 16, 1898; September 3,4, 1901.
Mancos Times, 1893-96. "Wetherill and Alamo Ranch" Manuscript, Mesa Verde National Park; 1893-98; July 6, 1900; June 21, 28, September 6, 1901.
Mancos Times-Tribune, May 18, and June 15, 1906.
Montezuma Journal, 1903, 1906.
Morning Democrat. December 15, 1897.
Rocky Mountain News, Oct 28, 1899.

Correspondence
Wm. Leonard to the Secretary of the Interior, October 29, 1906, Mesa Verde Archives.

Other
Durango Board of Trade Minutes, Center of Southwest Studies, Fort Lewis College, Durango, Colorado.
Mesa Verde Pamphlet, Denver: Carson-Harper, 1897c, Mesa Verde NP.
Minnie Hickman interview, June 16, 1982, Mesa Verde National Park.
Lee Kelly interview, Cortez Public Library.

3

1907-1919
Travails
for the Timid Tourist

By Duane A. Smith

Mesa Verde National Park

First wagon into Mesa Verde National Park circa 1913.

D espite expectations of increased tourism, financial betterment, and substantial gains in the "way of advertising by the entire surrounding country," plenty still needed to be done to attract tourists to Mesa Verde National Park. Better hotel accommodations within the park, improved roads and trails, and stabilization and preservation of the cliff dwellings would be a start. Cleaning and beautifying the grounds was another must. The litter of nearly 20 years' visitation lay scattered and blown about the Spruce Tree House campsite and wherever else people had wandered.

Work started almost immediately on several fronts. Archaeologist Jesse Fewkes, who had worked to create the park, made plans for stabilization in 1907. He employed laborers to "clear away the rubbish left by camping parties," and put the grounds around Spruce Tree House in "proper condition." He further issued orders that "no rubbish would be allowed to accumulate about camps or in the vicinity of the principal ruins."

Meanwhile, Hans Randolph, the first permanent superintendent, tackled two other tourist needs – a wagon road into the park and a reservoir for water. Both were vital to Mesa Verde's development. The *Denver Time*s (August 11, 1907) held out great hope for the park once such developments finally occurred. The "timid traveler," the reporter believed, found

Mesa Verde National Park

Jesse Fewkes

Mesa Verde almost inaccessible under present conditions. However, with improvement of the "torturous trail system" into good roads, and then, "in time," hotels with "creature comforts" the "weary wayfarer" would come. "Then indeed will the Mesa Verde National Park be second to none in the country; not even the far-famed Yellowstone park."

The reporter did caution that such progress should "not destroy [the] picturesque effect of the ruins," an apprehension that would echo down the decades that followed. Balancing the tourists' experience and enjoyment against the preservation of the park would be an ongoing and vital issue.

Randolph also found himself confronted by another issue that continued to haunt all the superintendents who followed him, finances. Lack of funds forced postponement of water supply improvements until the next fiscal year. The budget was short of money for surveying the wagon road and road construction, so Randolph took money from the amount appropriated for excavation and preservation to complete what he could. Building a lodge for visitors was postponed until appropriations were set aside, which would be awhile. Additionally, Randolph explained to Washington that "labor is at a premium in this country – hard to secure at any price."

Washington was none too happy with the superintendent shifting money around. He received a letter forcefully stating the Interior Department's position. While "recognizing the desirability of the early construction of good roads," the department pointed out, the park's principal purpose was "preserving and protecting the prehistoric ruins thereon." The department did not think it "advisable to depart from the plan outlined" for spending $2,000 to preserve and repair the ruins.

Mancos followed the road building progress with great interest. A small group of men worked into the late fall "trail making." They would improve those trails to road status, "to the entire satisfaction of Uncle Sam's constructing engineer," as "soon" as the government provided funds. By late November, weather suspended work because the "risk to life and limb is too great owing to the mixture of ice and snow in gorges facing northern slopes."

Despite financial and weather setbacks work went ahead the next year. The Mancos *Times-Tribune* (May 8, 1908) was pleased that surveying of roads and trails had been completed. Construction would begin soon, it hopefully anticipated, as well as development of a water supply. The paper predicted the park would be the "scene of much activity until the first snow fly of the next winter season."

"Soon" did not come as quickly as hoped. The surveyors looked for a new route with less than the 18 percent grade anticipated on a planned road. They found one, around the west side of Point Lookout, which came to replace the older Wetherill trail down the Mancos Canyon. Whether the next generation of drivers thought it was an improvement will be discussed later.

The Mancos newspaper promoted the route. In its June 5, 1908, edition, a reporter raved about what the tourists would see as they climbed toward the mesa. It promised to be one of the most "delightful as well as one of the most scenic of the entire section." The future promised to be even better. "When the Montezuma valley reaches a maturer stage of development there will be no more commanding view or a more beautiful scene than can be enjoyed in taking a trip to the Park." This part of the trip, rhapsodized the writer, would make the visit to the park "alone worth one's while," besides the "wonders" of Mesa Verde National Park. Who, among the traveling public, would not enjoy such an experience?

In spite of improvements, Fewkes expressed concern in his 1908 report that the park was accessed only by improperly constructed horse trails that were "in bad condition." He told all who read his report that building a road for carriages and other vehicles "is absolutely necessary if Mesa Verde park is ever to fulfill the purposes for which it was created." Comparatively few travelers "are willing to undertake the long and difficult horseback ride up the steep and dangerous trail." Further, the costs of conducting excavation and improvements were "very great because of the lack of a suitable highway." He suggested the government build a wagon route to the "ancient ruins upon the mesa."

By the time Fewkes' report reached Washington, that process had been started, yet his apprehensions highlighted a real concern over whether the park would ever be easily accessible for visitors. Randolph concurred and continued the road building. Finances continued to be limited, and economical and prudent use of funds remained the superintendent's goal. At least in the eyes of the *Times-Tribune* (September 3, 1909), he succeeded. An "immense amount of good work was done." By the "careful use of funds one mile of the most difficult part of the road" was almost completed.

The arrival of Secretary of the Interior, James R. Garfield, created quite a local stir when he and his party arrived on a special train in August 1908. They toured the park and the Secretary "expressed unqualified approval" of the work being done and the park overall. Like his father, President James Garfield, he was "much interested" in museums and the science of archaeology. At least the *Times-Tribune* (August 7, 1908) reported it that way. Perhaps more important, the reporter added that Garfield's visit "means a great deal to future park development" and consequently to "Mancos and this vicinity as well."

Courtesy *A Summer Outing*

The "Splendid Government Highway" into Mesa Verde, 1916.

But increased visitation also meant increased problems for the rangers and superintendent. "Laws and regulations" were published in 1908 to guide and warn visitors of "do's and don'ts." Among the constraints, visitors were "forbidden to injure or disturb mineral deposits, ruins, wonders, relics" and the like. The definition of "wonders" may have left a huge gray area in their minds. Campers had to settle in designated spots and "all garbage and refuse must be deposited in places where not offensive to the eye or contaminate any water supply in the park." They should start fires only when necessary and where they could obtain wood. The sale of intoxicating liquors was strictly forbidden. No excuses, persons violating the rules or guilty of "obnoxious, disorderly conduct or bad behavior" would be removed.

All this excitement and development bypassed Cortez, but not Durango and Mancos. Durango gained pass-through visitors, some of whom stayed for a day or two. Mancos, however, gained the most.

The *Times-Tribune* (May 15, 1908) gave an indication of the financial windfall. One local man received the recently awarded contract for two cisterns and a reservoir. Another had just completed the survey of the proposed roads and trails. A crew of about 30 men was "outfitting" to go with Jesse Fewkes to join 25 already excavating. Concluded the paper, "when they left, the town seemed half depopulated." When the appropriation for building roads and trails became available others planned to join in that project. Added to the money tourists spent for room, board, souvenirs, guided tours, and whatever else pleased them, Mancos did very well indeed.

Even Sterl Thomas, who had once guided out of Cortez, moved to his

THRILLS FOR TOURISTS

In Mesa Verde's first years as a national park, visitors sometimes had unexpected experiences. Eva Anderson, for example, left a breathless account of her drop into Balcony House in 1907. After climbing the "greased pole," an old tree trunk with its limbs chopped, she reached an upper ledge where she took a rest to "view the landscape o'er."

She and all other visitors went down the "rope." Tied to a cedar tree "projecting from a crevice far above us," she braced for her descent. "Nearly everyone hesitates - the guides encourage us" and well they had to because a several hundred-foot drop to the bottom of the canyon raised concerns. With one guide at the top and another at the bottom, Eva started down. "One climbs by means of the rope and small hollows chipped in the precipitous wall." Then she toured Balcony House.

Mesa Verde National Park

Climb down to Cliff Palace.

> We wander long in these apartments, often pursing [pursuing] some course, climbing over walls, crawling through narrow openings only, at last, to come up against a blank wall with no recourse but [to] retrace our path.
> All these dwellings are absolutely rifled of everything portable. [earlier, she disappointedly found only "some broken pieces of pottery and a flint arrow head" at the Spruce Tree House]

Then came the descent out. Eva slid down the rope while the guides admonished, "Hang onto the rope, hang on the rope." This priceless comment followed. "I wouldn't let go of that rope for all the wealth of Standard Oil."

Whether or not Eva's description of a trip into Balcony House encouraged the timid to come may be doubted, but it unquestionably excited the more adventuresome. She did make an interesting observation. While discussing the need for a new road, along with an up-to-date hotel, she felt it probable that an "ascent may yet be made in a touring car."

She hoped that would happen. On the day she started into the park, rain "was beating mercilessly against the window. Of course they won't go," Eva speculated. They did, in a wagon, and "I received a new lesson in western indifference to weather conditions. Indeed I've concluded that nothing but death stops a Coloradoan when he wants to go anywhere." She went 15 miles by wagon, and the remaining 10 by horseback, arriving at Kelly's cabin at five o'clock.

rival. "Mancos," he told the paper, "is the best place between Utah and the Mississippi River." As if to mimic the lyrics of that popular tune, "there'll be a hot time in the old town tonight," Mancos rocked ahead. To the *Times-Tribune*, "the old town assumed very much its former appearance in the days of the mining boom." Locals, especially, beamed when Mesa Verde pamphlets continued recommending Mancos as "the preferable starting point for the ruins."

Despite such enthusiasm from the press, the connection still needed to be made from valley to mesa top, a project not as simply done as said. Randolph, like Fewkes, never stopped reminding his Washington superiors of the crying need for park road improvements. He used some of the same arguments. Only those capable of the "rather trying horseback trip" came and therefore, travel to the park suffered because of the lack of a wagon road. Additionally, the expense of excavations, supplies, and materials and improvement overall "are very great because of the lack of a suitable highway."

In 1910, he pointed out that the carriage road ended at the foot of the mesa. A carriage road constructed on the top of the mesa would be easily and inexpensively constructed. Horse trails connecting it to the most important ruins could then be rapidly converted into carriage roads. All that awaited a carriage road to the mesa top, a major need. Unfortunately, building it would be neither inexpensive nor easy. Nor was that the only transportation problem facing visitors. Randolph pointed out that making it convenient to visit the interesting ruins in the western part of the park posed another problem because of the depth of the canyons cutting through the mesa.

While he continued to press for building roads and improving the water supply, Randolph added the need for a telephone and the creation of a local museum in the park. Having the nearest phone 25 miles away in Mancos obviously presented a major inconvenience.

His commendable idea for a museum faced one major obstacle. The ongoing collection and removal of relics by individuals and museums over the past nearly 20 years had left very little to exhibit. While future excavations would find relics, nevertheless, those that were easy to find had long since wandered off to other museums, private homes, and businesses. For the moment, a museum would have to wait.

The water issue also worried Fewkes, Randolph, and future superintendents. It had continually bedeviled visitors since they first arrived back in the 1890s. The "natural water supply is quite limited" and "entirely insufficient for future use," Fewkes warned. His 1908 report recommended a dam at the head of Spruce Tree Canyon to store water and construction of cisterns at available springs, particularly at the Spruce Tree spring.

From 1100 to 1300, as many as several thousand people are believed to have lived in the Mesa Verde area, a population that would not have been possible without an adequate supply of water. Now, in the early 20th century, a far smaller number of new inhabitants and visitors faced the chal-

C.B. Kelly and part of his "string" at Mancos Livery.

lenge of finding and storing sufficient water. Perhaps the amount of available water had changed through the centuries, and certainly people in the 20th century used more water than Ancestral Puebloans did. But ultimately, scarcity of water is believed to have been a factor in persuading the residents of Mesa Verde to leave the area.

Park employees built the dam Fewkes recommended and used the water primarily for pack and saddle animals. For human consumption the Spruce Tree House spring gained a cistern, along with an unspecified number of cisterns placed elsewhere in Mesa Verde. That matched current needs unless a drought or seasonal lack of rainfall interfered, neither an impossibility at Mesa Verde. Increased numbers of people visiting the park would surely put pressure on the water supply, however.

As the superintendents and the government struggled to ease the trip into the park and improve amenities at Spruce Tree House, visitor numbers slowly increased despite, as yet, no passable road for anything but horses. The Mancos newspaper generally hailed these determined adventurers and added a comment or two. For instance, the June 11, 1909, issue greeted Professor Emory Smiley and four other Durango teachers, and four guests, who toured the park. "They were a jolly crew which is evidence that the trip will not be lacking in point of merrymaking as well as scenic interest."

Charles Kelly, who had replaced the now departed Wetherills as the principal Mancos guide, charged $15 for one person or $12.50 apiece for two or more, for the three-day visit. His trips left at 7:30 in the morning and reached the Spruce Tree camp the same day. As a special attraction in the summer of 1909, archaeologist Jesse Fewkes gave brief lectures about the ruins at the site of his excavation work. Fewkes, a good speaker with a very romantic vision of the early mesa occupants, must have given his listeners a good show. He continued with his talks while he worked at various other sites in Mesa Verde. Before long, regular guided tours also would be available; on an informal basis, some already were.

Visitors continued taking a toll on the ruins as they scrambled about and, avoiding the best efforts of the park rangers, collected their souvenirs. Despite endeavors to clean the park, they thoughtlessly littered and had other impacts on the environment. Trees were cut for firewood, plants trampled by people and horses. Drainages were altered, causing erosion problems. As the second decade of the 20th century opened, plans and efforts continued to improve the quality of the visit, while Mancos and Durango mapped out how to make more money during the tourists' stay in southwestern Colorado.

There remained doubters who questioned the viability of Mesa Verde as a park. At a September 1911 national park conference in Yellowstone, one R. B. Marshall, possessing the title of chief geographer, let loose a blast.

> There is nothing in this park to make it of national importance save the cliff dwellings. There is no opportunity for camping: the scenery is common to many Western states and needs no protection. The inaccessibility of the park, the long distance, and the miserable railroad accommodations make it, I think, out of the question to make this park popular to any degree in comparison with other parks.

He went on to complain that "practically" no water could be found within the park and until it could be found, the Interior Department took a "big chance wasting public money" building roads and accommodations "the public may not be able to use because of that lack of water." Marshall recommended creation of "a national monument of small acreage around the ruins – say each canyon containing the cliff houses and have the area around all the canyons converted into a national forest." As could be imagined, those comments did not sit well with the friends of Mesa Verde. They wasted little time in replying with a spirited defense of their park and all its assets.

> Mesa Verde Park has wonderful possibilities for development. If properly provided for and effectively administered it should rank among the most important of the national reservations, a position which its quaint and mystic contents, its natural beauty, and its historical value fully justifies.

Then there surfaced those romantic views that completely contradicted

Marshall's harsh evaluation. "The ever-present mystery of the Mesa Verde, its picturesque location and invigorating air combine to make a stay in this National Park one of the most enjoyable experiences of a lifetime." A novice reading these conflicting views must have wondered if the authors talked about the same place.

Marshall, in truth, did not stand alone in his views. Among the American public, most of whom had never seen or stayed in a national park, people did question the expense of operations, the denial of the public's right to exploit the resources, and the apparent need to cater to the wealthy. Factoring time and distance, they appeared to be the only people who could afford, and had the leisure time, to travel the long distance from the East to such places as Yellowstone, Yosemite, and Mesa Verde.

Travel to Mesa Verde National Park, as well as inside it, remained impossible for most people. Roads leading to southwestern Colorado and to the park cried for help. Colorado had not done well funding roads. In fact, from 1889 through 1911, the state had appropriated no money for those roads leading into the region and only minor amounts for Montezuma and La Plata county roads. The more populated eastern slope counties received the greatest share of the money, a problem that only grew with time. Meanwhile, Americans lobbied for better roads, forming associations to that end, and pressuring Congress. The *Durango Herald* enthusiastically supported the "good roads movement." With a pinch of enthusiastic overstatement, it claimed in its July 12, 1913, issue that "citizenship suffers from poor roads." Good roads would increase church attendance and produce larger contributions and also improve schools! Sorry to say, it did not work out that way.

Neither was the enthusiasm of Superintendent Thomas Rickner's 1915 report borne out. "All the roads in the park have been worked, and in most cases widened and improved, until this drive from Mancos to Spruce Tree Camp has been termed 'The boulevard of the southwest'." The coming generation of motorists would have a bone to pick with Rickner and his "boulevard."

Washington eventually came to the aid of motorists. It had to. Some people had condemned the automobile because it "tore up" the roads and objected to "their" tax money being used to support this "destroyer." Counties and states struggled to keep up with maintenance that seemed to cost more with each passing year. This bind completely overtaxed the states' resources and did nothing to help the rural areas. The Lincoln Highway, which had just been marked out from coast to coast with great expectations, and other projects, needed aid that only Uncle Sam could finance. The result, the Federal Highway Act of 1916, enabled the construction and improvement of roads by federal grants on a matching basis with state appropriations. "Dollar matching," it would be called, and along with it came the acceptance of federal regulations.

Congress knew little about the cost of road building when it made an initial appropriation of $5 million, but soon found out a great deal. A start had been made but construction would not end in the lifetime of the great-great-grandchildren of people who cheered that start. For southwestern Colorado and Mesa Verde, federal involvement in roads held great promise, the best yet.

Durango embraced the dream of better roads, envisioning itself as a "pivotal point" for tourists with four "auto roads" radiating out from the Animas Valley to Farmington, Denver, Grand Junction, and Mesa Verde and Cortez. With Colorado's "finest scenic attractions" and the "best" fishing, hunting, and camping, the *Herald* could hardly estimate the value of good roads to the local scene. With a splendid road to Denver, the paper forecast, motorists could make the trip "in three days or less if in a rush." That time came sooner than the reporter probably expected as days of travel eventually shrank to hours. Even the most optimistic might have been hard-pressed to realize how quickly that would occur.

"THE NEW 'MOVING PICTURE MACHINES' HAD ALREADY CAUSED THE PARK SOME TRIALS DESPITE THE FACT IT MIGHT BE GOOD TO ADVERTISE MESA VERDE."

Travelers achieved the "three days or less" goal just before World War I. The 1917 park pamphlet advised readers that two routes from Denver could reach Mesa Verde. "A night is usually spent en route, and the ruins are reached by wagon, horseback, or automobile from Mancos." A night from Denver! Twenty years earlier, some people leaving Mancos spent a night camping before reaching the heart of the cliff dwellings!

As access to Mesa Verde improved, a new player entered the game in 1916, one that would reach a much wider audience of potential visitors. The newly created National Park Service sprinted into action to promote its parks, Mesa Verde benefiting with all the rest. The publicity landslide included essays, press releases, and more than a thousand articles by the end of the decade. Add to this pamphlets, road maps, motion pictures, and literature circulated without cost to schools, clubs and other groups over the country. Promotion soared and the public became aware, as never before, of their national parks and monuments.

The new "moving picture machines" had already caused the park some trials despite the fact it might be good to advertise Mesa Verde. Initially in 1911, the Department of the Interior stated that producers of films "for commercial purposes" must take "out a special license." The rate would be determined individually. Three years later the Durango Film Producing Company asked for permission to "make moving pictures of the scenery, ruins and other points of interest." What came of that is not known, but the next year lecturer Burton Homes asked to take motion pictures. This led to some unspecified crisis and a letter to Superintendent Rickner from an Interior official. "This whole moving picture business last summer lacked definite organization, and I am not trying to straighten out the tangle." Movies must await another time, but one that was not far away.

The Denver & Rio Grande also did its part to promote Mesa Verde. In 1916, it published "A Summer Outing Amidst the Cliff Dwelling Ruins in Mesa Verde National Park." The author, Methodist minister Elmer Higley, left no flowery phrases on the sidelines in enticing his readers to visit this "interesting locality, where once a mysterious people built up their rude civilization, flourished, and then faded into forgetfulness long before the Spaniards, 'zealous for God and a-thirst for gold,' crossed the unknown sea."

Denver & Rio Grande Railroad published this brochure in 1916.

He praised the recreation, "roaming through the canons, exploring the crumbing ruins, climbing the mesas," and the scenery. "Here is scenery, lofty mountain ranges, surpassing Alpine vistas, for the lover of the picturesque. Here are endless varieties of mountain flowers..." From Mancos, he wrote, the visitor journeyed into the cliff dwellings "over the new Government highway, recently completed and at an expense of $86,000. A two hours' ride, bringing into view alternating scenes of deep canons and distant mountains, terminates in a welcome sight of Spruce Tree Camp." Fear not adventuresome traveler, you will find "ample provisions made for our entertainment."

Higley assured readers that having finally reached the park, their efforts would be amply rewarded. "What a field for exploration, for study, for recreation! And then, too, what a field to take home with one from his summer's outing for reflecting visitation, deriving endless profit in awakened interest, and endless pleasure in happy remembrance." All this, concluded Frank Wadleigh, passenger traffic manager for the D&RG, offered a bargain. "The cost of an outing in Mesa Verde National Park is very moderate."

Further, in an advertising program for the winter of 1917-18, the railroad printed a brochure of the national parks and monuments along its route. The railroad also promoted a motion picture that included footage of Mesa Verde.

Such boosterism was not unusual or unexpected. Railroads had been involved in promotion of parks since the first one neared Yellowstone in the 1880s and the Santa Fe Railroad built a spur line to Grand Canyon nearly 20 years before it became a park, helping make it a "must see." Lobbyists for the Great Northern Railroad actually helped in the campaign to create Glacier National Park. Some became much more involved with the parks than what happened at Mesa Verde, operating hotels and scheduling excursion trains, for example.

The private sector joined in with travel books, motion pictures, and articles. Both before and after World War I, the public formed highway associations to pioneer in promoting construction of good roads and in publicizing what could be seen and enjoyed along them. Many passed near national parks. Southwestern Coloradans tarried not a step behind. To promote the area, locals joined the Spanish Trail Association, a regional group whose main themes were good roads and promotion of southern Colorado's abundant benefits. "Good roads are undoubtedly the prime factor of life and prosperity for every community" as travel by "motor vehicles comes into more general use." Mancos' *Times-Tribune* (August 24, 1917) had long agreed such ideas were well worth supporting. "With good highways connecting with the east and west, Southwest Colorado would soon become one of the favorite haunts of summer tourists in America." The Association managed to secure designation of the state highway leading into La Plata County and on to Mesa Verde and Cortez as the Spanish Trail. La Plata County, at the same time, gained the distinction of being "one of the leaders" in the construction of good roads.

More people would be coming because, among other things, park promotion did increase. The trip, still primitive, presented advantages for those determined to venture forth. The *Denver Times*, for instance, told its readers, the trip "gives an excellent opportunity to test the simple life, with plenty of rough and heavy climbing thrown in." These "pioneers" could expect plain food and "primitive accommodations" at the ruins. They should "wear old clothes and heavy shoes" and be used to horseback riding. Another publication suggested sturdy clothes and sweaters would "come in handy" on the cool nights.

The Department of Interior, in its 1915 park pamphlet, seconded those ideas. "Wear rough-and-ready outing garb – khaki suits and stout-soled, comfortable shoes will prove excellent. Ladies should wear divided skirts, as there are many ladders and steep trails to climb in getting in and out of the cliff ruins." The "climate is mild," but the nights "are cool" and extra wraps "will come in handy." The pamphlet assured the timid reader, however, that "many excursions in the National Park can be taken in perfect safety and comfort."

Esma Rickner and her sister worked at Mesa Verde during the nineteen-teens. She remembered the tents with board floors and "no heat. [The campers] didn't need it." One wonders about the recommendation of needing a sweater! The dining hall had a certain air about it as "a cedar tree went up through the middle."

Mancos applauded the *Times'* conclusion that it was the best place to go to start into the park. But "another way to reach" the park came through Dolores or Cortez. "Cortez had a fairly good hotel" and its guides charged about the same rate. Mancos begged to disagree. Interestingly, Dolores, also situated on the Rio Grande Southern railroad route, had not been considered a starting point before, since it sat even farther away from the park than its two neighbors and had not actively tried to secure a share of the tourism.

No matter where they started, visitors saw improvements each year. Stabilization of the major ruins went on over the next few years and soon Spruce Tree House, Cliff Palace, and Balcony House had been "improved" to enhance the visitor's appreciation of the sites and prehistoric culture. Fewkes and other archaeologists busily worked on these projects. The Secretary of the Interior, meanwhile, instructed superintendents to cooperate with the archaeologists in "every possible way." The superintendents' main focus, however, continued to be on such matters as building roads and trails, stopping vandalism, improving tourists' experience, and maintaining the park.

Spruce Tree House remained the camping site as it had been since the Wetherills' days. From there, visitors spent a day touring, their guide offering them a variety of places to see. Picking up "souvenirs" continued to be a problem and kept rangers on the alert.

Location of the park headquarters proved a contentious issue. For best protection of the ruins, a site within the park near the major cliff dwellings seemed most appropriate. But politics intervened, rearing its boondoggle head, and selection of a site became a political matter along with the appointment of superintendents and many rangers. With the superintendents coming from the Mancos area, little doubt existed. It was a foregone conclusion the headquarters should be located there. Mancos benefited immeasurably when it gained, and held onto, the headquarters.

All this effort to attract more of the touring public paid dividends. In

Brochure published in 1915 by
Denver & Rio Grande Railroad

1910, 250 people had visited, more than three times what it had been earlier. Promotion continued unabated, attracting even more tourists. The Denver & Rio Grande continued its efforts, helping immeasurably. It quickly published a pamphlet "Ancient Ruins of the Southwest" to help advertise what to see and its handmaiden, the Rio Grande Southern, offered reduced summer rates. In 1915, the D&RG sent out leaflets daily – 20,000 in a three-week period – and provided authors with information for articles. One of the more interesting efforts entailed sending 15,000 leaflets to college professors, apparently for them to mention the park to their students.

Articles continued to be published about the park by visitors, journalists, scholars, and writers giving varied reasons why this was a wonderful place to tour. Enos Mills, the "father" of Rocky Mountain National Park, visited Mesa Verde in 1915. He looked back on the trip with satisfaction and pleasure and wrote to the superintendent, "I have commended your work highly to the 'powers that be.' I gave both the Associated Press and the *Denver Post* an interview that will call attention to this park. This interview may not have gotten out correctly, nevertheless as it has been printed, it is excellent publicity."

Mesa Verde had come a long way as the second decade of the century moved along, and still had a distance to go before travel into the park became easy and convenient for all visitors. The same held true for staying within the park. Many folks did not enjoy camping and the facilities at Spruce Tree House had not improved much over Kelly's cabin of the 1890s, although tents, in a way, gave more privacy.

Writing in 1917, veteran traveler and author Eugene Parsons was "astonished so many Coloradoans never visited Mesa Verde." Here it sat almost at their doorstep and they "do not appreciate the opportunity that is theirs for a pleasure excursion of a few hundred miles." This would bring them to the "wonders" easterners travel thousands of miles to see. Probably for many eastern slope Colorado city dwellers, the idea of "roughing" it so "far" from home held little appeal. They may have fought to create the park, but many wanted more amenities and ease of travel before they ventured into it.

Closer to the park, though, southwestern Coloradans no longer worried about the government taking land for parks and forests or having too much government regulation overall. Those views had ebbed as the small trickle of tourists provided economic benefits which would not have come otherwise. The locals also gained an appreciation for what the 1917 park pamphlet proclaimed, "Remember that THE NATIONAL PARKS BELONG TO YOU." While maybe that appreciation meant only dollars, it was a start.

As Mesa Verde approached the end of its first decade as a national park, the park service and others made recommendations for changes and improvements. One change threatened Mancos' future with the idea of moving the park headquarters into the park. Superintendent Samuel Shoemaker sketched a plan that included erecting "proper buildings" at the mouth of Spruce Tree Canyon. He envisioned 60 acres of "beautiful land" improved and made into lawns, gardens, a hotel, concessions and various other buildings. "I can not too urgently recommend the building of a headquarters for the park on the site proposed and the removal of the office from Mancos at an early date."

The Department of the Interior took the idea under advisement. Fortunately for the water supply and the local environment, some of his recommendations fell by the wayside, but not all. Putting the headquarters in the park would strengthen federal control, aid in preventing vandalism, and potentially improve the public's experience.

Other recommendations also appeared, including the continuing necessity of a phone line to the park from the Mancos to Cortez line some 16½ miles away. Superintendent after superintendent continued pleading for more funds. Writing Congressman Edward Taylor, Thomas Rickner in 1914 had summarized the needs completely. "As you are aware, we have put off and put off from year to year until the improvement of the park has become a joke and people here are skeptical about anything being done to make the Park what it should be."

Four events changed the destiny of Mesa Verde National Park in the short span of two years, 1914 to 1916. Completion of the first road all the way into the park came first. Then the initial automobile caravan reached Spruce Tree House in 1914. In 1916, the National Park Service was created, and in the same year, the road over Wolf Creek Pass opened, offering the most direct route into southwestern Colorado. Few people, at the time, understood or appreciated the sweeping impact these four events would

Mesa Verde National Park

First automobiles, May 28, 1914.

have on the park and the region. The first two, road and cars, were tied together.

The automobile hard-chugged into southwestern Colorado around the turn of the century, but like wagons and carriages could not get into Mesa Verde because there was no road. At its January 14, 1914, meeting the Mancos Commercial Club proclaimed the great need for the park that "overshadows all others is the completion of an adequate highway into the Park, and, especially is it important, that this highway be completed as early in the spring as possible." They got their wish.

That long desired connection – Rickner's "boulevard" – was finally completed in 1914. The dream of the women of the Cliff Dwellings Association had been realized at last, a "safe road and a scenic highway not equaled in any state in the Union." Some minor adjustments still had to be made because of rock slides, narrow stretches that needed widening, and curves that had to be straightened a little, but it reached the road on the top of the mesa and soon the first horse-drawn wagon arrived. On "old dobbin's" tail chugged the automobile. On May 19, the initial "auto trip" of six cars, driven by locals, climbed into the park ahead of the official opening day of June 20. A daylong trip was reduced to hours.

These pioneering "automobilists" arrived when mechanics and gas stations were few and far between outside of larger cities. If a car broke down, the driver had to "get out and get under," as a popular song stated. Also, motorists in many areas could not find road signs, which were virtually nonexistent at this early date. Locals knew where they were going and others had to stop and ask the way.

The arrival of the car brought with it new regulations. The *Durango*

Democrat (June 19, 1914) advised readers that regulations had arrived from Washington governing the admission of automobiles. Drivers must secure written permission from the park office at Mancos and the fee was $1 per trip or $5 for the season. Automobilists should arrive no earlier than 6 a.m. nor later than 7 p.m. and when horse teams approached the motor vehicle was required to take a position on the outer edge of the road and stop. When nearing a curve, the driver must signal with his horn. Even speed limits arrived – 6 mph coming into the park, and no faster than 15 mph on the mesa top, unless approaching a horse team when it had to be reduced to 8 mph.

Not all the rules pertained to humans. Man's best friend, when taken through the park, "must be prevented from chasing animals and birds or annoying passersby." To this end, "they must be carried in wagons or led behind them while traveling." With cars that latter suggestion became outdated! When the family stopped, canines had to be kept under control or in camp. To make those points abundantly clear, "any dog found at large in disregard of these instructions will be killed." Hopefully, either the dog or the master could read. Tough on Fido, certainly, but better than his rival Midnight the cat. Uncle Sam did not even allow felines in the park.

Worried about more than cats and dogs, park regulations turned to drivers. A 1915 park pamphlet warned drivers coming into Mesa Verde, both those using horses and those driving autos, "the trip over the Government road should be taken only by parties who are experienced" in handling horses and driving. It "should not be attempted in season when rainfall in quantity occurs. All strangers traversing this route should be accompanied by an experienced guide." Reassuringly, the warning concluded "however the road at present, with careful driving, is perfectly safe."

Enterprising Mancosites promptly switched from horses to automobiles. Charles Kelly, once the Wetherills' rival and then the main guide, now owned, with a partner, an "auto livery." For $25 for one or two riders ($5 for each additional passenger to the "limit of the car"), he offered a one-day trip. The three-day horse trip faded into history.

Durangoans, too, wanted to offer trips to Mesa Verde. Superintendent Rickner recommended garage owners be "permitted to make trips to accommodate residents once a week on Saturday" for the "convenience of that city and vicinity." Such service would not be to the detriment "of our transportation concessioner," he believed. The Department of the Interior concurred "provided it is carefully watched by you and your officers."

Old dobbin retained the right-of-way for the moment, but not for long. Livery stable owners in Mancos might protest letting cars barge into the park, but it was to no avail. Rickner reported that "now very few horse-drawn vehicles" entered the park and, coincidentally, a "smaller number of tourists come in by rail." The nearby towns responded by offering "well-kept automobile" camps, as did the park, or so they claimed. These were needed because more than half the motorists carried their own supplies

Mesa Verde National Park

Phone box on Entrance Highway, west side of Point Lookout, circa 1916.

and camp equipment.

One thing the automobilists needed, and did not get for a while, was an "automobile map" of the park. That was understandable. Some intra-park trails could not yet handle cars, nor did the rangers want unsupervised visitors driving around here and there.

However, doing just that came more easily now. The superintendent's 1915 report proudly proclaimed, "all the roads in the park have been worked, and in most cases widened and improved," which meant plowed and graded. Rickner's "boulevard" would lead the public right into the park and on to the ruins. Rangers might be worried, but automobiles and motorcycles were allowed to make unescorted runs "to the ruins," which proved to be a bad precedent.

Despite such worries, Rickner predicted an increase in tourism and he was right. It more than doubled in 1916, breaking the 1,000 visitor barrier for the first time. Of course, accidents came along with cars. The *Times-Tribune* (September 7, 1917) reported the first fatality when a car hit a "boulder" and overturned 2½ times killing the driver. Also, people felt the automobile made it "absolutely necessary" that the long-sought phone line be completed. Money to extend the line finally was diverted from the excavation and repair budget.

The phone company placed five boxes along the road, thus never leaving the traveler far "beyond the use of the long distance telephone." These phones connected calls to the Mancos exchange. More than just a convenience, they provided a comforting safety connection to the outside world should a car break down or an accident occur.

"FIRST AUTOMOBILE CLUB RUN TO THE MESA VERDE NATIONAL PARK," shouted the *Semi Weekly Durango Herald* (September 10, 1917), following with a long account of the adventure. "A dozen or more Oldsmobile car owners" started from Denver on Saturday, September 1. Coming via Poncha Pass and the "new road over Wolf Creek pass" they reached Pagosa Springs on Monday afternoon. This exciting venture caught headlines and local attention. Here we pick up the story elaborated with a bit of colorful prose and follow along.

Center of Southwest Studies, Fort Lewis College, Durango

Highway between Durango and Mesa Verde, circa 1926.

A phone message carried the news of their presence at Pagosa to Durango and the fact that they would continual [continue] their journey at the hour of 3 p.m. It was then that the Durango Exchange, members of the daily press and others arranged an auto party for the purpose of meeting the Denver visitors some ten miles east of Durango and escorting them into the city, where they were to remain for the night, supply their cars and prepare for their journey to Mesa Verde.

On Tuesday morning the San Juan sun arose as usual in all his glory. The wonder seekers gathered themselves together, refilled gasoline tanks and supplied themselves with other necessaries of the auto tourists and by the hour of 10 a.m. had lined up along lower Main avenue.

The reporter could hardly contain himself. "... a jollier set of boys and girls, men and women you will never expect to see together on any occasion. All realized that they were out for a good time and there was never any doubt about it."

> The distance of 30 miles from Durango to Mancos was made in less than two hours. All enjoyed the beautiful scenery as they passed up Hesperus hill land thru Thompson's park ...
> By the time the party had reached Mancos, secured their government permits to enter the park, it was realized that all agreed upon one thing and that was that it would be well for them to take a lunch before leaving the beautiful city of Mancos with which all the visitors had fallen in love.

Then the pace picked up because they wanted to see Virginia McClurg's pageant at Spruce Tree House that afternoon.

> All autos were tuned and times [timed] and the race for Spruce Tree house began... Before many minutes passed they had reached the entrance to the park eight miles beyond Mancos and then began the most wonderful drive which cannot be surpassed on this continent or even in the mountains of the Alps. As they passed along the beautiful government road which led them steadily and rapidly upward to the mesa land 2,500 feet above, the minds of all were filled with wonderment. It was the grandest moment of their lives.

Four days out of Denver and an hour and 45 minutes from Mancos "the cars rolled into the beautiful parking place – constructed and supervised by the government [superintendent] Thomas Rickner." They made it in time for the pageant "a representation of the early lives of the ancient Cliff Dwellers based upon the myths and legends concerning those people." On the return trip, they left via Durango, Trimble Hot Springs, enjoying a dip and dinner, Silverton, and Ouray.

This was such an extraordinary event that a reporter went with them. Awesome at the time, it more than hinted at the future.

The automobile club members certainly seemed to enjoy their trip over Wolf Creek without any undue problems. Automobilists were becoming much more adventuresome!

The park, too, joined the new automobile world in 1919. Superintendent Rickner purchased a Ford sedan for $1,119.37. The vehicle included a tool box, "special shock absorbers," an electric starter, and wheels with "demountable rims."

The third of the four developments that significantly swayed Mesa Verde's future came with the opening of Wolf Creek Pass. Before that time, the fastest way to reach Denver and the east remained the train, a day and a half journey

Mesa Verde National Park

The Kelly-French Stage, Morefield Canyon, circa 1916-18.

on the indisputable king of the road. No direct roads ran between Durango and eastern slope Colorado towns. One possibility did exist, at least, to cross the first high mountains east of Pagosa Springs and journey to the San Luis Valley and beyond. But Elwood Pass, near the future Wolf Creek Pass, was a terribly rough and steep road crossing and it had become barely passable after a 1913 flood. No one ventured over it in winter. Except for local travel, only a few hardy souls attempted longer journeys via the fledgling public road system.

All that potentially changed in 1916 with completion of the U.S. Highway over Wolf Creek Pass, at a cost of about $100,000. Opened with an appropriate ceremony on August 21, the steep, gravel, one-lane road, with occasional turnouts for passing vehicles, promised a better future for the region and Mesa Verde. Not that it meant an easy drive by any stretch of the imagination. Cars coming up had the right-of-way and those coming down had to back up to the nearest turnout, which was not an easy experience. When the snow flew, which could be early in fall on occasion, the pass closed. Cars with gravity flow gas tanks sometimes had to back up if the gas supply ran low. The same thing could happen on the precipitous road into Mesa Verde, particularly with its average 8 percent grade. It took a skilled driver to safely back around curves and uphill.

Despite being an improvement, Wolf Creek did not resolve all the problems. Drivers unused to mountain driving found it quite formidable, as the superintendent's monthly report in October 1919 noted. Tourists would have come if snows had not "already blocked the road." He wished there were another way "into and out of this section." A road ran from Ouray and Grand Junction but to get there from Durango the driver went through the San Juan Mountains and crossed over several 10,000-foot passes which proved as formidable for cars as Wolf Creek Pass. New Mexico, which had just gained statehood in 1912, did not as yet have a decent public road system in its northern counties. To be sure, a car caravan from Los Angeles managed, with a great deal of trouble, to reach Durango in 1911, a pioneering venture that Durangoans followed almost like an expedition in darkest Africa. Beyond Flagstaff, Arizona, they drove almost in no-man's land. Nothing significant developed from their trailblazing venture.

Superintendent Rickner correctly foresaw that the opening of the road would bring many eastern tourists, and Wolf Creek definitely was a major factor in 1917's increased visitation. Admitting that the road was both new and rough, he believed a great future lay ahead when it would be improved and better known to the traveling public instate and out-of-state. With typical local pride, Rickner wrote that scenery through "which the road runs is the finest in the State."

The fourth development that directly impacted the park came with the creation of the National Park Service. By the mid-teens, 16 national parks and 18 national monuments had been set aside. For years a growing apprehension existed about management of these national treasures, especially when they became political playthings with the appointments of superintendents, for example. The evolving conservation/environment movement also became involved with such figures as John Muir and groups like the Sierra Club joining the debate over the best management and use of the parks and monuments. Worried about the fate of such national jewels being lost among the pressing variety of demands upon the Department of the Interior, reformers lobbied for a separate organization.

With some logic and much emotion, they argued that parks could be best served in the hands of their friends. Under a separate organization, parks and monuments would encourage economic growth through tourism and beneficially give Americans a healthy escape from urban and industrial areas. In reality, Mesa Verde hardly matched favorably with this idea, being too far from urban areas to provide convenient escape.

Interest in the governance and future of parks was only part of a larger crusade. Starting in the early 1900s, the Progressive movement gained momentum and Americans became reform-minded on a host of matters, from woman's suffrage to trusts, as they called the threat of big business.

Park enthusiasts and conservationists won their battle. Two men, Stephen Mather and Horace Albright, who would play roles at Mesa Verde, and others helped draft the legislation and lobbied for its passage. Eventually, the park advocates saw their goal accomplished in 1916 and obtained their own bureaucracy in Washington as a bureau of the Department of the Interior. The act directed the park service "to conserve the scenery and the natural and historic objects and the wildlife" and provide for their public use.

Particularly significant in Mesa Verde's case, the act also charged the service to use such means "as will leave them unimpaired for the enjoyment of future generations." The age and delicate nature of the Ancestral Puebloan ruins made this goal particularly imperative. Preserving the past for the enjoyment of the present and future would shape Mesa Verde's heritage.

That tension between use and preservation marked an ongoing saga at Mesa Verde. Nothing loomed more critically for the future. Now the park had a new "boss." Mather became the first director of the Park Service and Albright his chief assistant.

The average visitor did not take time to consider what the park service might or might not accomplish. A museum, after a decade-long discussion, finally opened in 1917, in an old log cabin. As Superintendent Rickner wrote the director of the park service two years before, "it has been a matter of wonder to tourists, and a disappointment to them, there was no collection" for them to see. The Denver & Rio Grande Railroad helped the project along "with a remarkable series of pictures of natural features in the park and ruins." While other museums had better exhibits, thanks to earlier collecting, at least a start had been made and the modest museum represented the first in the national parks. Two years earlier, Jesse Fewkes' occasional talks had become regular, inaugurating campfire talks. Visitors could now gain added insights into the prehistoric peoples and ongoing archaeological work.

Future improvements came with installation of an "electric-lighting plant" that provided sufficient power to light the entire tent camp at Spruce Tree House. Previously, campers used lanterns – more romantic perhaps! Visitors did not have to rent a tent; they could bring in their own outfits.

Reading the park pamphlet may have induced many of them to do just that. After discussing the beauty and the views of this "different" country, the park service snuck in this little gem: "There is a fairly comfortable camp near Spruce Tree House."

After a visit to the park in 1917, Horace Albright made some recommendations to concessioner Oddie Jeep, wife of a park ranger. To improve the visitor's stay, he wrote, each tent should contain a bed, dresser, straight chair, washbowl and pitcher, slop jar, large rug, towels, dishes, and so forth. If this were done, then he would authorize an increase in rates to $4 per day. If not, "on the other hand, I do not feel justified in permitting you to change from the $3 per day rate." The $3 already represented a jump from 75 cents for lodging and 75 cents for meals in 1915. Add to that the $1 fee for a single trip, or $5 "for the season," for "automobiles and motor cycles," and it was becoming more costly to visit the park.

Albright, according to the *Denver Post* (October 28, 1917) had come to Mesa Verde with a "feeling of indifference." Like many others, he departed with a changed opinion. He went back east to tell his friends about the "country of the wonders to be found." The rival *Denver Times* (September 14, 1917) quoted him with even more favorable opinions. Albright placed the park "in the front rank of the world's most magnificent scenic wonders. It has a distinction all its own that is not possessed by any other of the national parks." Both papers hoped it would finally receive the government attention it "long deserved" and the region would be advertised.

For the moment, though, the country's attention was focused elsewhere. Mesa Verde did not exist in a vacuum. The outside world could, and did, come crashing down on the park. World War I cut tourism as the federal government discouraged recreational travel. Excavations stopped too, as Washington used the money for war-related expenses. Rickner commented to Fewkes there were many things they wished done in the way of preservation, "but, of course, while the war lasts, little can be done along those lines."

Patriotism was the call of the day. The government encouraged park employees to buy liberty bonds as they did Americans everywhere. "I know that you will do every thing in your power to persuade the men and women under your jurisdiction to purchase at least one $50 bond," explained a letter from the Department of the Interior.

War needs also increased pressure to open parks for cattle and sheep grazing and timber cutting, the latter not a problem at Mesa Verde. Albright warned his superintendents about this threat, but the war ended before it became reality.

As the second decade of the 20th century came to a close, Mesa Verde sat poised for a tourist boom. Almost all the pieces had fallen together. The long desired road into the park had become a reality; the automobile had navigated the curves and grades; a better road to the east opened; and a new bureaucracy focusing solely on national parks guided its destiny. Unequivocally, problems remained. The Four Corners' isolation hurt and so did the park's distance from urban population centers. How much? Rocky Mountain National Park, Colorado's second (1915), had an estimated 51,000 visitors the next year and was soon leading all national parks in attendance (1919) with 170,000. It easily surpassed the older and famed Yellowstone National Park which reached 62,000 in 1919. That showed what ease of access and population concentration could provide. In contrast, Mesa Verde hit a record of 2,287 that year and would top 3,000 a couple of years later.

While Mesa Verde would never have such advantages as Rocky Mountain National Park, it presented a great deal of untapped potential. The lack of decent roads to the west and south still limited potential travelers from southern California, Arizona, Texas, and beyond. Even neighboring Utah and New Mexico fared little better.

Where did the visitors come from? Rickner had a count of 371 private cars that entered the park in 1918. Two hundred eighty-five came from Colorado, 23 from New Mexico, 15 from Kansas, and 11 from Utah. No other state topped 10 and only Illinois and New York registered visitors from east of the Mississippi, most people reluctant to travel that far. Demonstrating the problem of not having an acceptable and direct route

Mesa Verde National Park

Campfire talk in 1915. Jesse Fewkes is seated fifth from the left.

to the west, none arrived from California and only four from Arizona. When a group of visitors arrived from Brooklyn the next year, it created quite a stir and even gained a mention in the annual park service's report.

Without blinking, Mancos' *Times-Tribune* (July 25, 1919) proclaimed, "Mancos is the Tourist Town of the southwest. Pass the word along." The editor, nonetheless, understood Mancos needed more attractions for tourists. The year before (August 30, 1918), he suggested "something in the way of sports and side trips" should be developed. The park should not be the end of the road "and Mancos only a gasoline station. Think about it."

After tourists bought their gas and continued into the park, they found better accommodations than ever before. Their experience was also superior to their parents' because of the museum and its exhibits, campfire talks, better interpretation about the history and the sites, and more stabilized and preserved ruins.

Mesa Verde's attendance had improved with the opening of Wolf Creek Pass and Americans' growing love affair with the automobile. Attendance in 1917 had topped 2,000 for the first time, then leveled off with the impact of World War I. Then it started to grow steadily again. Local residents and towns hoped the trend would continue as America returned to peace-time pursuits. With two national parks now, Colorado envisioned itself becoming a "center of the tourist industry." The new decade promised to be an interesting one.

SOURCES

Books
Fewkes, Jesse, *Reports of the Mesa Verde National Park* (Washington: Government Printing Office, 1908): 6; 10-11.
Wiley, Marion, *The High Road* (Denver: State Department of Highways, 1976): 9; 15.

Articles
Anderson, Eva, "A Tenderfoot at the Cliff Dwellings of Mesa Verde," *The Chautauquan* (July 1908): 194, 202-04.
Beam, George, *The Prehistoric Cliff Dwellings of Mesa Verde* (Denver: George L. Beam, 1916(?)): 2.
Blodgett, Peter, "Selling Scenery," *Seeing and Being Seen: Tourism in the American West* (Lawrence: University of Kansas Press, 2001): 275-77, 282, & 285.
Parsons, Eugene, "Prehistoric Ruins in Colorado," *Pleasureland* (December 1917): 3.
Unidentified newspaper clipping, August 24, 1906, Mesa Verde National Park archives.

Publications
Denver Times, August 11, 1907.
Durango Herald, July 12, 24, 1913.
Mancos Times-Tribune, September 13, 1907; August 30, October 25, November 1, 29, 1907; May 15, 22, 29, 1908; September 3, 1909.
Times-Herald, August 9, 16, 1918.

Correspondence
Horace Albright to Mrs. Jeep, May 24, 1918, Mesa Verde correspondence file.
Ina Allein to Author, June 3, 1998.
D&RG to Rickner, October 19, 25, 1915, correspondence file, Mesa Verde archives.
Department of the Interior to Rickner, April 17, 1918, correspondence file, Mesa Verde archives.
_____, to Rickner, May 25, 1918, and Mancos Commercial Club, January 14, 1914, Mesa Verde archives.
_____, to Wright, July 27, 1911; to Rickner, December 11, 1914; May 10, & December 10, 1915, Mesa Verde archives.
Stephen Mather to Rickner, October 20, 1915, Mesa Verde correspondence file.
Enos Mills to Rickner, September 20, 1915, correspondence file, Mesa Verde archives.
Jesse Nusbaum memo undated, Superintendent File, Mesa Verde archives.
Thomas Rickner to Fewkes, July 27, 1918, Mesa Verde correspondence file.
_____, to Edward Taylor, no date, 1914, William Winkler Collection.

_____, to Secretary of the Interior, February 13, 1914.
Secretary of the Interior to Randolph, October 25, 1907, Mesa Verde National Park archives.

Other
1909 Mesa Verde pamphlet, Manuscript Collection, Mesa Verde National Park.
A Summer Outing Amidst the Cliff Dwelling Ruins in Mesa Verde National Park Colorado (Denver: Carson Press, c1916).
Annual Report of the Department of the Interior (Washington Government Printing Office, 1919): 16-17.
Esma Rickner Bauer Interview, April 23, 1982, Mesa Verde Oral History archives.
Colorado Yearbook for 1918 (Denver: ??): 124.
Copy of the concessionaire agreement, May 1, 1913, author's possession.
Cummings, Densil, "Social and Economic History of Southwestern Colorado, 1860-1940," Unpublished PhD Dissertation, University of Texas, 1951, 497-505.
Report of the Director of the National Park Service (Washington: Government Printing Office, 1918): 73.
How to Reach the Ancient Cliff Dwellings (Denver: Carson-Harper, 1916): 2.
Louisa Jensen to author, November 5, 1998.
Mesa Verde National Park (Washington: Government Printing Office, 1915): 5-6.
_____, (1917): 19.
National Park Service Annual Report (Washington: Government Printing Office, 1918); 16.
The Prehistoric Cliff Dwellings: Mesa Verde National Park, i, & 28.
Proceedings of the National Park Conference...September 11 & 12, 1911 (Washington: Government Printing Office, 1912): 110-16 & 174.
Randolph, Hans, *Report of the Superintendent* (Washington: Government Printing Office, 1909, 1910), both reports page 7.
_____, *The Prehistoric Cliff Dwellings: Mesa Verde National Park* (Washington: Government Printing Office, 1915): i.
_____, *The Mesa Verde National Park* (Washington: Government Printing Office, 1917), 19.
Thomas Rickner, *Reports to the Department of the Interior* (Washington: Government Printing Office, 1917): 817.
_____, "Report of the Superintendent, 1918), *Reports of the Department of the Interior* (Washington: Government Printing Office, 1918): 169; 167.
Shoemaker, Samuel, *Reports of the Department of the Interior* (Washington: Government Printing Office, 1913): 710, 712.
Superintendents Annual Reports - 1914, 1917, 1918 & 1919; 1915, pages 3 & 5, Mesa Verde archives.
Wright, William, *Report of the Acting Superintendent ...* (Washington: Government Printing Office, 1911): 10.

4

Tourists by the Carload

By Duane A. Smith

Mesa Verde National Park

An accident on Knife Edge Road, 1925. A National Park Service car is pictured on the right.

A transformation came to the park in 1921, one that was probably unnoticed by tourists visiting Mesa Verde, yet would be greatly understood by nearby communities. Heralding a new era, for the first time a trained archaeologist was appointed superintendent, Jesse Nusbaum. The 34-year-old Coloradan had been involved with excavation and preservation at Mesa Verde and held some decided opinions about what needed to be done to improve the park and the quality of tourists' visits. In a series of sweeping memos and letters, he laid out what he saw as problems and challenges, and his plans for addressing them.

Within a month, he wrote the park service about a potpourri of problems. The sanitary arrangements, public and private, "are distressingly bad," inadequate in size, and not well kept. Nor did Nusbaum like the road into the park with its "excessive grades, twenty to thirty percent" for short stretches and a large number of "excessively sharp switch backs." The roads from the camp to the various ruins "are too narrow and winding for the safety of automobile traffic" and should be gradually widened. In all of these, he echoed earlier superintendents' concerns and complaints.

The first help came with completion of the infamous Knife Edge road in 1923, some five miles shorter, and less steep than the previous one around Point Lookout. It pleased Nusbaum, "the road alone should double the attractiveness of this park." Many who drove on the new road voiced

Mesa Verde National Park

From left, Dewitt Wilcox, Jesse Nusbaum and Deric Nusbaum in 1929.

decidedly different opinions.

Ina Allein remembered her father driving the Knife Edge. "There were stations on it with a phone connection to Mancos. At each the vehicle [driver] called & asked if the next station was clear, repeated at each. They'd wait if a connection wasn't clear." She also recalled that "a Ford car had to back up three mile hill for traction."

The public camp, Nusbaum believed, had been intentionally built in a "remote, bad location," with no water and all valuable firewood taken way. With no signs directing people to the site, visitors were essentially forced to "patronize" the concessioner's lodge. Commingling in a very small area overlooking Spruce Tree House was the concessioner's property – dining room, kitchen and eight single room frame cabins with 74 tents – and government property, including quarters for rangers and others and the museum. Simply finding a place to park sometimes presented a huge problem.

Nor did he like the guided tours and their lack of professionalism. The children or in-laws of the concessioner and government employees who conducted them jumped on the running boards of "every visitor's car and proffered services as interpretative guides for a fee." The chief ranger's 5-year-old son had a signed poster at the log cabin museum "stating he is the best guide" and knew all about archaeology. "The interpretive story these kids (5 to 12 or 13 years of age) told the visitors was out of this world." Kids and people climbed over and photographed ruins and picked up shards as souvenirs. There seemed to be almost no direction or control. The underlying cause of all this, in Nusbaum's eyes, rested with Chief Ranger Fred Jeep, his wife Oddie, and their family who managed to have their fingers in all these activities.

To correct this, Nusbaum found himself taking on the local political establishment that had so long considered Mesa Verde National Park their chief "loaves and fishes" from government patronage. He believed Jeep, Rickner, and their cronies lurked behind the accusations that his new policies were harming locals. The fight eventually carried all the way to Washington and a meeting with Senator Lawrence Phipps, who, according to Nusbaum, told the superintendent, "it's your responsibility to attend to Republican lines in that region and let the ranger run the Park." With the help of National Park Service Director Stephen Mather, Nusbaum straightened out that mess and professionalism triumphed in Mesa Verde. Nusbaum achieved his goal. "We are to win out, put this park in the best shape possible and make every visitor a continual booster for it."

In a sense, all that was a mere warm-up in the "bullpen" before Nusbaum really entered the game. He decided to move the park headquarters into the park, a plan considered for years. His reasons were simple – convenience, best utilization of time and money, better administration, and ease in excavation and protection of the ruins. Those reasons failed to sway Mancos folks and the superintendent had a fight on his hands. For Mancos, being the headquarters was the most prestigious thing the community could claim and not a small economic windfall.

Moving swiftly, Nusbaum opened the headquarters near Spruce Tree House in 1921, started constructing buildings, and, for the first time in the park's history, park administrators stayed at Mesa Verde all year. Reminiscent of the "old days," it took three days for pack and saddle horses to make a round trip to Mancos for mail and supplies in the winter when roads were not kept open. The park still opened only seasonally, May 15 to November 1. Winter weather shut the roads and ended tourism, the park having no equipment to battle the snow. A driver did not want to, or should not have wanted to, risk life, passengers, and car on the steep, ice- and snow-covered roads into and throughout the park.

Moving park headquarters from Mancos marked the end of the community's dominance over Mesa Verde tourism. The crown had rested uneasily on the town for years. Now Mancos became a pass-through point rather than a destination. There existed no real reason to stop there except, perhaps, for food or gas. It lost to rival Durango, ending the more than two-decade battle over which town would dominate Mesa Verde tourism.

Durango had nearly eight times the population, and offered more

Mesa Verde National Park

A touring car that was part of Beers "stage" line. George Anderson was the driver.

hotels, businesses, and restaurants, more amenities, and more activities for visitors. In that day and time, when automobile travel might mean an adventure of flat tires and car problems, it had more gas stations and auto mechanics as well.

The town also led with a strong and active chamber of commerce (called the Durango Exchange at that time), the best in the region, which relentlessly promoted Durango, "Come to PLAY and you'll want to STAY." In one of the classic examples of their effort, the chamber produced a map that placed Mesa Verde right near Durango with nary a notation of Mancos. What Mancosites thought of that went publicly unrecorded!

Such activities, of course, angered neighbors who fought back to corral their share of the tourist trade. In 1934 several New Mexico cities warned against coming to Durango because of a water shortage. Indignant Durangoans could not believe a rival would stoop to such tactics! Even if Nusbaum had not moved the headquarters, Durango already had advanced well on the way to winning dominance over Mancos and its other neighbors.

Durango had more railroad connections to the region, an advantage that was fast receding. More importantly it had more highway outlets. It might take some doing, but an automobile could go north, west, and east, as well as south at least as far as Farmington. With very few exceptions, people traveling to Mancos by auto or rail came through Durango.

Mancos still offered the nearest rail connection, but the era of the train being tourists' principal transportation had retreated as rapidly as Mancos's crown. The demise of rail travel hurt the town almost as much as the headquarters move. Railroads had opened and linked the West and fostered tourism. Now the automobile raced to replace them. Already total rail mileage was shrinking and passenger travel declining. Parks like Yellowstone and Glacier that had once dominated in popularity because of railroad connections now found that the automobile made all parks almost equally accessible, except for distance and traveling time. Furthermore, old style accommodations built to match the expectations of the "elite" railroad visitors became outdated with the advent of auto campers.

The automobile, indeed, made tourism more democratic, no longer just for those who could afford the time and expense of a long western railroad adventure. Middle-class America could now travel to the parks with growing convenience and reasonable expense unknown in American history. The car brought people whose expectations differed from previous generations, increased the popularity of the parks, put mounting pressure on scenic and park resources, and produced expanding demands for services and even more parks.

The "automobilists" held other advantages over their predecessors of a decade or so ago. Just as Durango had more gas stations, so did other communities, making mechanics and even auto dealers easier to find. Road signs had improved as well in the 1920s, taking some anxieties out of the adventure.

The car also made another impact. For the touring public, hotels had been the places to stay. Usually located near a railroad depot or in the downtown, they had been a tourist feature in late 19th and early 20th century America. They did not, however, serve the needs of the new travelers well. Parking was limited, the location might be inconvenient from the highway, and they might be too expensive or too old. Better able to respond to the changing times, the auto court or motel arrived on the scene with parking and more convenient locations nearer the highways. Durango led the way in the Four Corners region and tourists would have no trouble finding one there. Another innovation, the auto camp, was even more economical if, perhaps, the travelers enjoyed pitching a tent, cooking meals, and sharing communal bathroom facilities.

Mancos clearly could not keep pace and join the "roaring" '20s as Americans took to the road. It could only watch disconsolately as autos whizzed by on their way to the park entrance, dollars flying away and never coming back. For the next generation Durango faced no serious competition for its role as the "gateway" to Mesa Verde National Park.

Visitors in the 1920s expected to be able to visit and tour the new superintendent's home while in the park. A Renaissance man, Nusbaum had planned and helped build the park headquarters buildings in an attractive, "early modified pueblo style." Tourists apparently looked upon his home as part of the park experience. Nusbaum asked Mather what to do about this unexpected development. Mather "fully realized" the "unique results" the building style had achieved, noting it could be a valuable tool from an "educational standpoint." Then he went on to remark, "on the other hand, a man's home is his castle and the superintendents of our parks and their families are entitled to, and should have, that privacy in their own homes that any other citizen is entitled to." Public inspections stopped.

On a more serious matter, Nusbaum tackled the long vexing problem of inadequate water that only magnified as visitation increased. By 1925, a grim water situation threatened the park's growing popularity. Construction started within the next two years on one-acre shallow catchment basins located on slopes and ringed with rock to hold water, a tactic used by the Ancestral Puebloans centuries before. A reservoir, plus storage tanks, completed the water system. That only temporarily resolved the problem and by the 1930s once again the park faced an acute water shortage. With rainfall unpredictable and too many acres potentially tied up with the project, attention then shifted to deep wells.

Ironically, too much rainfall hurt tourism as well. When the "monsoon" rains hit around August, roads became treacherous and slippery. Rock and mud slides proved particularly troublesome on the Knife Edge road. With a jolly sense of humor, Nusbaum reported to Washington, D.C., in 1929.

> The "Rain Gods" of the aboriginal inhabitants of this area, in complete control of the peak travel period, obliterated all travel gain of the earlier part of the season and were apparently not content to let the "Sun God" rule, even intermittently, until the end of the first week of September.

Dozens of cars "wallowing up the entrance through the mud turned back" when they saw only steep grades ahead that were "equally muddy." When all visitors saw "literal seas of mud," they became even more wary of that "infamous" entrance road, despite Nusbaum's claim that "the outlook from it is probably one of the finest in the world." Rain also hampered travelers coming over Wolf Creek Pass and other routes to the park, even closing the roads at times. It seemed that Mother Nature remained determined to cause problems one way or another.

Helen Wells Frahm remembered what rain could do, when interviewed 60 years after she took her first 1920s trip into the park. The "zigzag" road, as she described what was apparently Knife Edge, scared her to death during a rainstorm. "We slithered down that hill." She concluded, "it was very precarious to come up here."

Along Knife Edge, Nusbaum used army rifles to shoot down hanging rock slabs loosened by spring thaws. His staff did the same thing along the main trails for fear they "might kill or seriously injure visitors later in the spring." Injuries did occur. The list included, in June 1926, an injured foot, a bruised muscle, insect bites, a twisted ankle, something described as "throat gargle," an injured finger, and a car accident.

Should a tourist suffer such problems, Mesa Verde stood prepared, thanks mainly to Nusbaum's wife Aileen. Prior to the Nusbaums' time, the park had no medical facilities beyond a first aid kit or two. Realizing the grave need, the superintendent initially used a room in their home before purchasing a large tent and some medical supplies in 1922. His wife cared for the injured until he appointed a medical student as a temporary ranger.

Meanwhile, she started to raise funds for a small hospital and consulted authorities throughout the country on the design and necessary arrangements. Nusbaum hoped that some funds would come from the San Juan Basin because of local "great interest in the park," and "many visits." He contacted some of the women who had led the fight to establish the park, with unknown results. A congressional appropriation of $7,500 completed funding for the project in 1926. Named in her honor, the Aileen Nusbaum Hospital included an operating room, doctor's office, kitchen and three large rooms each with two beds for patients.

Employees paid a small fee, based upon their monthly earnings, to receive medical treatment. Hospital charges for visitors varied with their need from $3 to $15 for "operating room charges and dressings." The visiting public could feel a bit more at ease.

While hopefully most of them never needed the hospital's services it was available and so was another improvement, the upgraded museum. This they did enjoy. Determinedly and professionally, Nusbaum moved to improve that facility. With his wife's help, he had the old cabin completely "overhauled," and specimens cleaned and returned under "predetermined classification." In his eyes, the previous exhibits had been a "great confused jumble." To improve the park's collections, he encouraged people to return artifacts taken in the earlier days. Some did appear, making it more crucial that a permanent museum building be constructed. Neither Congress nor the National Park Service had available funds, so Nusbaum became a fundraiser. Without question, he excelled. In perhaps his greatest achievement, he succeeded in getting John D. Rockefeller, Jr., interested in Mesa Verde. Their partnership would touch various aspects of the park for years to come.

Money came not only for a building, but for excavation of one of the mesa top ruins to add to the exhibits. With the museum finished and the exhibits displayed in a professional manner, Nusbaum personally turned to expanding the park's collections. During the winter months from 1924 into 1929, he excavated ruins in remote areas of the park, occasionally working through the "torn-up refuse of earlier diggers."

All this added a new dimension for visitors and they seemed to appreciate his efforts to immeasurably improve the first museum in a national park. The real significance of Mesa Verde came with the educational experience the public received, not the scenic wonders that could be viewed, as

Mesa Verde National Park

Camping July 22, 1936.

fascinating as they might be. Nusbaum resolved to improve the exhibits and the information available to the best of his ability, thereby setting the foundation for all that would follow. Located on Chapin Mesa above Spruce Tree House, the museum conveniently served both the day visitor and those who stayed for a few days.

To improve the sightseers' edification even more, Nusbaum stopped the haphazard and wild guide service that had so appalled him. The 1923 Mesa Verde pamphlet clearly stated the time and place for tours each day. Private motorists should "congregate at the Camp Fire circle at 8 a.m. and 1 p.m. sharp" for ranger- and guide-led car trips to the various ruins. Rangers would assign parties "arriving late" to guided tours at 10:30 and 3:30 and because "of the large number of visitors, no deviation would be made from this schedule." The Park Service strictly "prohibited tipping" of rangers or guides. For the more adventuresome visitor, saddle horse and pack animal service "is available for those who wish to leave the beaten path and rough it."

Louisa Jensen, daughter of Buck Ames, the earlier concessioner, remembered a camping trip she took with her friend Myrtle Armstrong into the park in 1924. With a pup tent and a "stout wooden box with tight lid [holding] our food and cooking utensils," they camped between two juniper trees for shelter. "Daddy helped us select an area free of rocks, comparatively level, with a natural platform so that if it rained, water would not enter our space." The tourist lodge, at the time, contained a restaurant and also "sold some snack foods as well as items of general interest to tourists. If we tired of camp cooking we could go to the Lodge."

One day, they took a horseback trip. "The trip took from midmorning to midafternoon with a sack lunch eaten while stopped at noon on the trail. The primitive trail required surefooted horses." About 10 people rode on the trip. The two girls also visited other cliff dwellings on their own, something that Nusbaum would not have appreciated. Her father had "taught us" not to disturb anything, so all "debris was left as we found it for future inspections by experts."

She also mentioned going down a crude trail into Cliff Place numerous times because the family lived in Mancos and entertaining company from out of town usually included a trip to Mesa Verde.

> When returning to the top of the mesa a choice of path or rope was offered, I always chose the rope. This was nothing like present day rope climbing. We tied the rope around the waist, put our feet against the cliff face and 'walked' to the top where the ranger gave a hand to congratulate the climber until legs became steady once more. He then released the rope off the edge for the next climber.

Repeat visitors found something new from earlier days. The Spruce Tree camp – lodge, all tents, and cottages – had been moved to a slightly different location overlooking Spruce Tree and Navajo canyons. The old site nearer the ruins simply could not be enlarged and with 60 percent of the visitors crowding into the campground facilities, a change became imperative.

Tourists using the free public campground, which was finally properly signed, received instructions to leave "your camp clean when you leave the park." Campers were admonished to use the limited water supply "sparingly and help conserve." Bathing in the reservoirs was "strictly prohibited" and wood for fuel could be "taken only from dead or fallen trees." Cats, at last, gained their revenge with dogs joining them as *non grata* in the park. Dogs were permitted "only for those persons passing through the park to territory beyond," and had to be "kept tied while crossing the park." No camping with man's best friend would take place, despite the most tearful pleas.

The public also found rates moving upward. Two people or more in a tent cost $3.75 per day, or $15.50 per week, including meals. Single meals cost $1 and a bath in the bathhouse 50 cents. That was for adults; "children under eight, half of the above rates." For those more adventuresome souls, a horse trip including a horse of "gentle western stock," lunch, can-

Mesa Verde National Park

Conoco Travel Bureau Bus, June 1934.

teen, slicker, and a guide cost $6 for one person or $3.50 each for three or more riders. Ladies who had not come prepared to rough it might rent divided skirts for only 50 cents per day.

The Park Service continued to worry about inexperienced or over-confident motorists. Drivers were warned to take precautions before considering entering the park. They should "satisfy" themselves that both the foot and emergency brakes "are properly adjusted to stop and hold a car on any grade." At the very least, there had to be six gallons of gas in the tank, the radiator had to be filled with water, and the crank case had to contain oil to the "proper level." For those unfamiliar with mountain driving, the "ascending machine had the right of way," and the descending vehicle had to back up to a place where the cars could pass.

Once in the park, they were warned about the effect of the "high altitude" on cars. More gas would be used and power reduced, not to mention overheating the engine at 7,000 or so feet. Drivers also generally should utilize "one gear lower" on steeper grades "than would be used in other places."

For those not wanting to challenge the Knife Edge, the Mesa Verde Transportation Company out of Mancos (with a never-say-die spirit, it still claimed to be the "gateway to Mesa Verde") did the driving. The same company, working through Western Slope Motors, operated daily "motor service" leaving Grand Junction at 6:45 a.m. and stopping at Delta, Montrose, Ouray, Silverton, and Durango, the "metropolis of southwestern

Colorado," before arriving at the park at 7 p.m. The Mesa Verde Transportation Company held a franchise to take tourists into the park and charged, depending on the starting place and number of people transported, from $11.50 to $46.50 for a round trip.

The company did not like competition and protested when the Denver & Rio Grande promoted itself and Durango. "[The Mesa Verde Transportation Company] cannot see any reason why it is necessary for the D&RG to operate into Mesa Verde." It did no good. Durango also provided transportation which did not help matters in the company's eyes.

Tourists had other opportunities depending upon their pocketbook and schedule. The Santa Fe Transportation Company, under the management of the Fred Harvey Company, conducted "motor cruises," known as the "Sierra Verde circle cruises" from Albuquerque, Santa Fe, and Taos. These took a week, cost $150 per person, and visited Chaco Canyon, Aztec, Taos, and Santa Fe. By 1927, Gallup also joined the group and three years later "cruises" arrived from Winslow, Arizona, although not on a regular basis. The Fred Harvey Company proudly claimed it operated hotels with "excellent accommodations" in all of the New Mexico communities mentioned. As roads were built or improved, competition mounted, but the key issue of distance still weighed heavily.

The Santa Fe railroad and the Fred Harvey Company had long wanted to tap the Mesa Verde market from Gallup, as had that community. Daunting miles over terrible roads, if they could be called that, had prevented all but a few from venturing northward. Then the government completed a highway, from fabled-in-song Route 66 which passed through Gallup, north to Shiprock in 1926. Designated Highway 666, it eventually extended into Colorado and Utah. That 666 designation, the biblical "number of the beast," troubled some people for the next 77 years until it was changed in 2003 to U.S. Highway 491. Beastly or not, people used it and Gallup jumped to corner its share of the tourists.

Once again competition grew, as in the old days. After a night's rest at Fred Harvey's "first class" El Navajo Hotel, the trip took a full day to reach the park. A day's visit followed, and then back to Gallup. The auto stage, which left on Mondays and Wednesdays, cost $40 and with it, Gallup assumed it would soon "become a very popular gateway." Shiprock gained a little as well, as it furnished the lunch stop both ways. For the first time, the Denver & Rio Grande faced a railroad rival in the Santa Fe, but alas, neither railroad found Harvey's enterprise any kind of bonanza. Their heyday had passed.

Nusbaum explained one reason why the Santa Fe railroad and Gallup did not reap the returns they wished. He, and they, had hoped the road would be a "great boon to this section, a feeder to the park," and increase travel to the area. But Colorado let him down, as Nusbaum found in a trip he took over the road.

Holding his speed to 55 mph, he had arrived in Shiprock, "with absolute comfort." New Mexico maintained the road from there to the Colorado state line, not yet part of the highway, in "excellent shape." Then the trouble started.

> [after] one hour of grief and ruts and chuck holes and bouncing all over the road to make the comparatively short distance to Cortez. For years everyone cursed the New Mexico end of the road, now they can curse Colorado and below Cortez unless it is more promptly and better maintained.

Nusbaum made the trip, but many visitors in their own cars did not care to tempt fate.

The superintendent and his fellow drivers were confronted by other problems as well. Ruts jostled cars back and forth. Sudden washouts left drivers stranded on the side of an arroyo that had not been there earlier. Embarrassingly for drivers, their fading competitor, the horse, pulled out cars stuck in mud, or mud-splattered humans pushed the car to drier ground. Gravel, too, could nick a window, dent a door, or scuff paint. Driving on the highways and byways of the Southwest took "pioneering" spunk.

If the tourist from the south had problems, so did the ones from the north in a little different manner. Those tourists saw "wonderful scenery," but had to cross over 10,000-foot passes, with curving roads, narrow ledges, and steep drop-offs that meant a scarier, "longer route" than many "cared to take." So that left Wolf Creek and the new southern routes as the best ways to come. Nusbaum, as superintendents before him, pleaded with the federal government to spend money on roads outside the park. Nevertheless, transcontinental routes crossed overland far away from the park where population centers held more political power and consequently gathered more than their share of highway spoils.

While the federal government provided limited overall help, Colorado was trying to do better than Nusbaum's experience suggested. Part of the problem resulted from their rather late involvement, since the state did not have a highway department until 1921. Then, most of its effort went to the more populous eastern slope.

By 1928, only 348 miles of paved highways existed in the whole state. Another 14,900 miles were surfaced with gravel and graded, or simply graded, but that left 68,000 miles of unimproved state and county roads. For the traveler such statistics provided little comfort or compensation. The road to Mesa Verde from anywhere included some trying times.

Still, tourists did come in increasing numbers, jumping to a decade-high peak in 1928 of 18,872. Improvement of the roads found more people coming from the Midwest and West, with the South a poor third. The East hardly made much headway, probably for the usual reasons of time and distance.

Such definite growth nevertheless paled in comparison with Rocky Mountain National Park that in the 1920s topped 100,000 visitors every year. That was the grand total for Mesa Verde from 1906 into 1930. Rocky Mountain National Park not only accommodated more visitors, it received more funds from the federal government. In the period 1917-29, for example, its appropriations totaled $781,671 compared with Mesa Verde's $362,506.

To overcome the isolation that still plagued the region, advertisement of Mesa Verde continued unabated. The Denver & Rio Grande did its share to boost declining passenger traffic. "Come into western Colorado, where a genuine western welcome awaits you at every hamlet, town and city." Its "Gems of Colorado Scenery" described how easy it was to reach the park from Mancos. Those efforts increased more at the end of 1929, when the railroad gained the concessioner's contract and a bus transportation contract for the park.

Dissatisfied with the tourist facilities at the park and the "bus line" out of Mancos, the D&RG planned a change. They organized the Mesa Verde Park Company as a subsidiary and set about to do better. One "innovation" came with their plan for tourists to take the main, standard gauge line to Grand Junction, then travel by bus to Mesa Verde. This would eliminate the "long round about trip" by narrow gauge from Alamosa to Mancos and shorten the trip "one full day."

Nusbaum did what he could by writing and speaking and he helped writers who needed Mesa Verde information. Local newspapers joined in as did Denver and New Mexico ones occasionally. Denver even harbored hopes of gaining a portion of the business from travelers to southwestern Colorado. The Denver Tourist and Publicity Bureau distributed promotional literature on behalf of Mesa Verde that served both the park's and bureau's interests. It proved a woebegone hope, however. Distance, weather, and poor roads cut into the capital city's aspirations. Despite this effort, many southwestern Coloradans believed that Denver neglected them, a long-held belief. Looking at where highway money went and paved roads started and ended, that idea seemed not too farfetched.

Another promotional breakthrough helped as well, movies. If Americans loved cars in the 1920s, they probably loved the movies even more. The Mancos *Times-Tribune* (July 2, 1926) praised the efforts of the Fox Film Corporation whose recently finished Mesa Verde film undoubtedly meant "broad advertising" and a "great boost for the park." The company took footage of ruins and park scenery and filmed part of a play that took place in Cliff Palace. The play supposedly told the legend of finding fire and a "number of Indians took part."

To a lesser degree another new wonder of the age offered new advertising possibilities in the early 1920s, the radio. By the end of the decade Americans had become "hooked." While it was difficult to receive major stations in the Four Corners because of distance and mountains, it would not be long before aggressive local stations emerged, vigorously plugging nearby features and events.

Nevertheless, more than isolation and hard traveling were accountable for keeping travelers away. Thomas Rickner had put his finger on the problem, which was about image. "For some unknown reason the large majority of tourists come to this park with the idea that it is a desert land, and that the journey is hard and uninteresting, over an arid, barren country, the ruins of the cliff dwellers the only point of interest." Coming in from the south across the Navajo reservation might have strengthened such an opinion. This "erroneous" view must be weighed against the fact that many people had come from more vegetated and tree-lined regions with abundant rainfall to support vegetation. Finding beauty in the desert takes time and understanding. Of course, reading many of the Mesa Verde articles would have convinced an unfamiliar person that this land was semi-arid at best.

Undaunted, they came. One 1936 visitor had nothing but pleasant memories. "In an atmosphere conducive to rest and relaxation" he found "many things of interest" to occupy his "time and mind." In a "Book of Impressions" maintained in the park, they also recorded their one-sentence opinions.

> A most interesting and educational park full of romance and thrills.

> The Cliff dwellings should be counted as one of the wonders of the world.

> I never expected to see anything so awe inspiring in the world.

> Good retreat for honeymooners. [Interesting idea!]

> There are no words that can express the beauty and do justice to Mesa Verde.

And then one person, who came in over the "million [dollar] highway" through the San Juans, offered his memories. "They told me this is the end of the 'Million Dollar' drive. Well, I got a million dollars worth before I got here and was ready to quit anytime. Here is where you sure get your money's worth."

The Million Dollar Highway this writer described ran from Ouray to Silverton then on to Durango with the last major link completed in 1920. It needed constant maintenance and with its narrowness and high passes scared probably more drivers than Knife Edge. Nonetheless, the park service thought it would become the "greatest inducement along with Mesa Verde" in bringing visitors to southwestern Colorado. They also believed Wolf Creek Pass would do the same and when everything fell into place, it

Hikers showing a variety of dress.

would be part of the shortest route from Denver to Los Angeles.

Lest it be thought that visitors did not complain at times, they did. Poor food or service, high prices, small portions of food, lack of cleanliness, miserable facilities, a scary road – the list stretched on, limited only by the individuals' perceptions and frustrations. Such concerns aside, most visitors enjoyed and learned at Mesa Verde.

Of course, some visitors left their mark and got caught. One Denver woman received this notification because of her "thoughtless act" of placing her name on the box cover above Square Tower ruin.

> The circumstance of finding your name and address at a prominent and much visited location of this national park will, I am certain, prove embarrassing for you. It is certainly disturbing to us. What sort of a park would we have if each visitor inscribed his name and address or his mark herein?

The "misdemeanor" cost $2 to sand and repaint, an expense the park expected her to pay.

The importance of Mesa Verde in attracting visitors to the region also gained more universal attention. Moab, Utah, became disgusted when no signs showed "our highway 450 leads quite directly" to the park. The Lions Club got busy and contacted civic clubs in Monticello, Blanding, and other Utah towns to join with them to get signs. They wanted the park to fund the idea, but while the superintendent considered it "a real opportunity," park funds could only be spent within the park. The Montrose, Colorado, chamber of commerce wanted visitors routed north to them as that, they claimed, offered the shortest route to Yellowstone!

Optimistically, visitors all got their million dollars' worth of enjoyment and profit before the era ended, in October 1929, after which the worldwide financial crash that multiplied into the Great Depression discouragingly dragged on for more than a decade. The "roaring" '20s went out with a whimper and the depressed early '30s did not promise any quick solutions to the nation's woes.

The situation only worsened as the years went by and the nation's economy hit bottom in 1932-33. Disgusted and frustrated with the Republican efforts to solve the crisis, the American public turned to the Democrats and Franklin Roosevelt, with his New Deal program. As a result of this multifaceted program, help arrived for the depressed Four Corners states and Mesa Verde National Park. Before the depression and the 1930s New Deal days became history, changes came that forever transformed the park and its neighbors. Not everyone agreed it was a step forward, but undeniably a watershed point had been crossed.

Visitors to Mesa Verde would have noticed changes very quickly. The boys of the Civilian Conservation Corps, one of the most popular New Deal programs aimed to help unemployed youth, worked on an assortment of projects. From the tourists' perspective, the CCC built museum dioramas, a popular addition completed in 1939. *Mesa Verde Notes* (December 1939) described what the staff hoped would happen. The dioramas would enable visitors to visualize the life and people of the cliff dwelling days. That in turn would allow modern folk to better understand and appreciate what they saw than was possible before the dioramas.

One visitor agreed wholeheartedly as reported in the same issue. "Looking back over the trip, one thing that impressed me most was the diorama sequence in your museum. As I said before, I have worked on models and dioramas and know the possibilities and perils. I feel you have the trump cards in your five small cases."

The CCC and the New Deal did more than that. They built buildings, ran surveys, constructed and worked on roads and trails, erected fences, excavated sites, made new parking lots, walks, water fountains, and overlooks, installed telephones, put power lines underground around the headquarters, built a new campfire circle for talks, catalogued the library collection, and landscaped. All this in one way or another benefited visitors who enjoyed these monuments to the productive CCC program.

Ansel F. Hall

Even more, it benefited the young men who worked at Mesa Verde as individuals, starting some on a lifelong interest in archaeology and the national parks.

The last CCC camp closed in May 1942, ending an amazing era. Other New Deal programs tackled as wide a spectrum of problems and needs. Those that contributed to Mesa Verde and the surrounding states included road construction and rebuilding, construction and improvement of airports, installation of lines for the Rural Electrification Administration, and government aid to Colorado and individual counties. The 1930s, however, also hurt the park in a host of ways, most notably in a leveling off of the number of visitors until 1936.

Why numbers turned upward at that point is open to speculation. The Great Depression eased somewhat, the economy stabilized, and public confidence started to return. Considering that gasoline remained cheap and some automobiles were relatively inexpensive to buy and operate, an auto vacation might have been a feasible way to relieve depression blues. The cost was lower particularly if the family camped out, which meant more work for mom and dad and great fun for the kids. With roads improving and campgrounds multiplying, a camping trip was within the reach of many American families. Mesa Verde offered all the necessary ingredients for a pleasurable and affordable trip – a low entrance fee, campgrounds, and educational experiences during the day and at the campfire talks at night, and different scenery than many people saw every day.

The depression severely curtailed the Denver & Rio Grande's plans for Mesa Verde, as did the continued loss of passenger traffic to the automobile. Despite a strong marketing program, and all the planning, the depression gloomily settled in and profits tumbled. Like many other companies, both that railroad and the Rio Grande Southern soon found themselves in trouble and bankrupt. The D&RG bailed out of Mesa Verde's concessioner business and concentrated on keeping itself afloat.

> "Hall planned changes, but the world situation dictated otherwise. By late 1939, World War II had broken out in Europe."

Ansel Hall, meanwhile, organized a company that took over the railroad's concessions company. Hall, a veteran park employee, an advocate of museums and education for the park visitors, and the chief naturalist of the park service for seven years, resigned his job – and a mandated transfer to Washington, D.C. – to take over the Mesa Verde concessions. A rare combination of "romantic idealist and practical businessman," Hall served as president and manager of operations until his death in 1962.

His main objective was to work in harmony with the park service to the "advantage of the visiting public." A quick survey of the accommodations at the park found that in the spring of 1937 approximately 125 guests could be housed in 40 tents and 27 cabins, "all without running water or any type of plumbing facilities" with a central bathhouse (two bathtubs) and a lodge building with a dining room. That summarized the total of all the physical improvements since the park had authorized the first tent camp back in 1911.

One of Hall's first innovations was a store carrying a "full stock of groceries, fresh meats, vegetables, fruits and eggs." Visitors had requested such a service for years and now they gained it, but during the park's six months of winter closing, the store depended on park employees' patronage. The superintendent sent out a memo encouraging just that, reminding them the store "merits your patronage."

Hall planned changes, but the world situation dictated otherwise. By late 1939, World War II had broken out in Europe and two years later, with the attack on Pearl Harbor, America joined the conflict. Tourism, for the duration of the war, with its gas rationing, tire shortages, and no new cars, collapsed back to the levels of the 1920s.

The last peacetime American season, 1941, saw visitation top 41,000. It dropped sharply to 13,000 the next year, and 4,000 in 1943. Before this happened, however, despite the depression '30s, two trends had emerged. Visitors arrived from all over. During the 1934 season, for example, cars came from every state in the union showing the impact of the automobile even in hard times. Also that year, tourists arrived from 24 foreign countries. Even in the 1939 season, with war near and then beginning, sightseers from 13 countries and all the states, plus Alaska, Hawaii, the Canal Zone, and the Philippine Islands, toured Mesa Verde. The director of the park service proclaimed, Mesa Verde "is fast becoming a place of national and international interest." He felt this reflected, in part, the "dissemination of the story of the prehistoric inhabitants among schools, homes, and abroad." Promotion definitely helped, yet it could have been added that improved roads into the park and accommodations within, and nearby, equally enticed visitors. Looking back to what it had been in 1920, the experience the public had at Mesa Verde from park road conditions to education to food and lodging improved immeasurably.

Another new form of transportation opened potential for park visitation, the airplane. Durango had an airfield and a few planes had actually brought tourists who then headed for Mesa Verde. What this might mean for the park, only the future would tell. Most Americans had never flown in a plane, let alone for any distance. The lion's share of the public looked upon air travel as quite exotic and an expensive way to get from here to there.

For whatever reasons, Mesa Verde was becoming better known and a visit to it a "must." Without question, the park still lagged far behind Rocky Mountain and Yellowstone in attendance and appropriations, and its relative isolation continued to hurt visitation. Its worth and significance, though, grew in both the public's and federal government's eyes.

SOURCES

Books
Nusbaum, Rosemary, *Tierra Dulce: Reminiscences from the Jesse Nusbaum Papers* (Santa Fe: Sun Stone Press, 1980): 72-74 & 234.
Rothman, Hal, *Devils Bargains* (Lawrence; University Press of Kansas, 1998): 38-39, 44, 47, 152-53, & 157.

Articles
Cook, Judy, "A History of the Civilian Conservation Corps at Mesa Verde National Park," unpublished paper, August 1984, Center of Southwest Studies, Fort Lewis College, Durango Colorado: 46-59 & 68.
Smith, Jack, "The Nusbaum Years," *Mesa Verde Occasional Papers* (October 1981): 11, 9-14, 23.

Publications
Denver Post, February 11, 1926.

Correspondence
1937 memo oil route 666, Road Outside Park file, Mesa Verde archives.
Ina Allein to author, July 15, 1998.
Clarkson to Nusbaum, August 23, 1927, correspondence file, Mesa Verde archives.
_____, to J. J. Downey, January 29, 1929,
Louisa Ames Jenson to Author, November 28, 1998.
R. E. Hauser to Leavitt, July 29, 1934, Road Outside Park file, Mesa Verde archives.
Stephen Mather to Nusbaum, January 31, 1925, correspondence file, Mesa Verde archives.
Mesa Verde Transportation Co. to Arno Crammer, May 7, 1927, correspondence file, Mesa Verde archives.
Nusbaum to Mather, June 9, 1921, correspondence file, and Nusbaum memos, superintendent file, Mesa Verde archives.
_____, to Boyer, August 11, 1922, correspondence file, Mesa Verde archives.
_____, to Surgeon General Hugh Cumming, March 12, 1925.
_____, to Mrs. O. Boyle, June 8, 1925, correspondence file, Mesa Verde archives.
A. E. Palen to Finnan, January 13, 1932, Road Outside Park file, Mesa Verde archives.
Acting superintendent Richard Wright to Secretary of the Interior, July 21, 1911, correspondence file, Mesa Verde archives.
Superintendent Memo, September 9, 1937, July 18, 1939, & August 6, 1940, Mesa Verde archives.

Other
Annual Report of the Secretary of the Interior (Washington: Government Printing Office, 1928): 179.
"Book of Impressions," Mesa Verde archives.
"Book of Memories" and Management File, Mesa Verde archives.
Civil Conservation Records, Mesa Verde archives.
Cliff Dweller, March 31, 1937.
Colorado Yearbook, 1928-29 (Denver: Bradford Robinson, 1929): 21l.
Concession agreement, May 1, 1930, Mesa Verde archives.
Helen Wells Frahm interview, February 9, 1981, Mesa Verde archives.
Mesa Verde National Park (Washington: Government Printing Office, 1923): 19.
_____, (Washington: Government Printing Office, 1930): 63 & 66.
National Park Service Annual Report (Washington: Government Printing Office, 1929): 25.
Mesa Verde Notes, December 1934 & December 1939.
Jesse Nusbaum speech, undated, Mesa Verde archives.
_____, "Report of the Superintendent, Report of the Director...1922 (Washington: Government Printing Office, 1922): 59.
_____, Reports, September 2, 1921, June 5, 1922, Mesa Verde archives.
_____, Report, March 3, 1922, Mesa Verde archives.
_____, "Report," August 4, 1921 & January 5, 1922, Mesa Verde archives.
_____, Report, June 1926, Mesa Verde archives.
_____, Report, 1929, Mesa Verde archives.
_____, "monthly report," February 1929, Mesa Verde archives.
Report November 12-13, 1935, meeting, Road Outside Park file, Mesa Verde archives.
Report of the Director of the National Park Service (Washington: Government Printing Office, 1922): 59; and 1923: 71, 73.
Report of the Director of the National Park Service (Washington: Government Printing Office, 1926): 45.
Report of the Director of the National Park Service (Washington: Government Printing Office, 1930): 120, 121, 126-127.
Thomas Rickner, "Superintendent Report," *Annual Report of the National Park Service* (Washington: Government Printing Office, 1920): 291.
Robert Rose, *Water Supply History of the Mesa Verde National Park* (Mesa Verde: Mesa Verde National Park, 1952): 19-20, 27, & 29.
Rules and Regulations Mesa Verde National Park (Washington: Government Printing Office, 1927): 6-7, 13-14, 51-56, & 60-61.
Schedule of hospital rates 1929, Mesa Verde archives.
William Winkler collection.

5

Postcards Welcome You to Mesa Verde

By Duane A. Smith

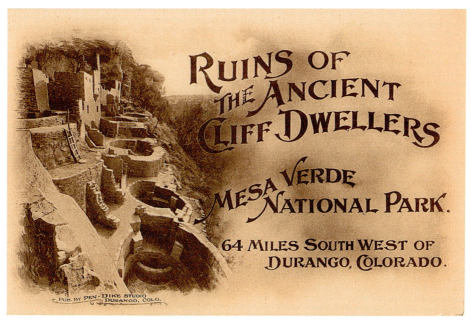

Center of Southwest Studies, Fort Lewis College/Nina Heald Webber Southwest Colorado Collection

Obviously no earlier than 1906, this postcard was published in Durango, showing that locals were not a step behind in making money off the tourists.

The popularity of postcards can never be doubted. Within six months after the federal government put them on sale, May 1, 1873, Americans purchased more than 60 million of them. These one-cent cards produced an almost immediate impact on writing style, as long flowery phrases gave way to terse comments crowded into limited space.

The government would not have a monopoly on these popular items for long; soon private companies entered the field. The first American pictorial postcard appeared in 1895. By the turn of the century, they had become all the "rage." Middle-class folk, at least, had more leisure time and sending a card home allowed others to share in the family travels. Buying them as souvenirs helped to retain memories.

Although not many people visited Mesa Verde in the early 1900s, black and white and colored postcards were there to greet them. The fad, which had started in Europe in the late 1860s, now had spread to southwestern Colorado. Enjoy the samples presented herein. Taking you past mid-century, these postcards are from the Nina Heald Webber Southwest Colorado Collection in the Center of Southwest Studies at Fort Lewis College.

William Henry Jackson took this photograph. By 1903, Jackson's Mesa Verde photographs had been around for a decade.

Though Mesa Verde was not a park when this card appeared, it gave tourists a way to show their friends how they "roughed" it while touring Cliff Palace.

96   P O S T C A R D S   W E L C O M E   Y O U   T O   M E S A   V E R D E

Center of Southwest Studies, Fort Lewis College/Nina Heald Webber Southwest Colorado Collection

This 1908 postcard provides an early view of Spruce Tree House before it was "cleaned up."

Visiting Balcony House provided a thrill, but not a 1,000-foot one! See the postcard caption.

Center of Southwest Studies, Fort Lewis College/Nina Heald Webber Southwest Colorado Collection

Lucy Peabody briefly had a monument for her efforts to create the park, but alas, it is now known as Square Tower House.

Imagine driving up this winding and steep road in your Model T! The first automobilists did just that in 1914.

Center of Southwest Studies, Fort Lewis College/Nina Heald Webber Southwest Colorado Collection

Center of Southwest Studies, Fort Lewis College/Nina Heald Webber Southwest Colorado Collection

Most visitors never saw the S. P. Thomas House, located in Spruce Canyon and named after an early guide.

Spruce Tree House had been stabilized by the time of this photograph, making it much more accessible for visitors from 1914 on.

Center of Southwest Studies, Fort Lewis College/Nina Heald Webber Southwest Colorado Collection

Center of Southwest Studies, Fort Lewis College/Nina Heald Webber Southwest Colorado Collection

Spruce Tree Camp was better than camping out, as the earlier visitors had done.

The Knife Edge road along the west side of Point Lookout scared visitors for years, until the present road replaced it in 1957.

Center of Southwest Studies, Fort Lewis College/Nina Heald Webber Southwest Colorado Collection

Center of Southwest Studies, Fort Lewis College/Nina Heald Webber Southwest Colorado Collection

By the 1920s, Mesa Verde was becoming a popular destination with more tourist amenities available.

Tourists who were afraid of heights must not have liked this overlook at Spruce Tree Camp.

Center of Southwest Studies, Fort Lewis College/Nina Heald Webber Southwest Colorado Collection

Despite the 1930s depression, more visitors saw Cliff Palace than ever before.

With a bit of romantic license, someone named this Speaker Chief Tower at Cliff Palace.

Center of Southwest Studies, Fort Lewis College/ Nina Heald Webber Southwest Colorado Collection

Many a visitor had second thoughts about climbing the ladders at Balcony House.

World War II was now history, and travel and visitation picked up as America enjoyed boom times.

Center of Southwest Studies, Fort Lewis College/Nina Heald Webber Southwest Colorado Collection

Center of Southwest Studies, Fort Lewis College/Nina Heald Webber Southwest Colorado Collection

Painted cards, as well as photographic cards, appealed to visitors. These two cards were painted by artist Paul Coze and published by Ansel Hall. There was a series of 24, in two sizes.

Spruce Tree Lodge looks quite western in this 1948 postcard.

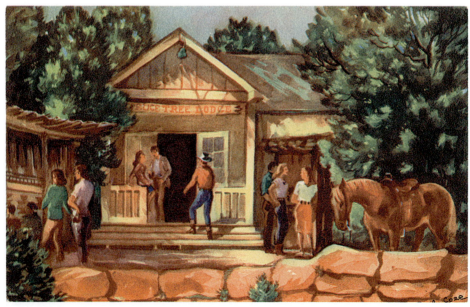

Center of Southwest Studies, Fort Lewis College/Nina Heald Webber Southwest Colorado Collection

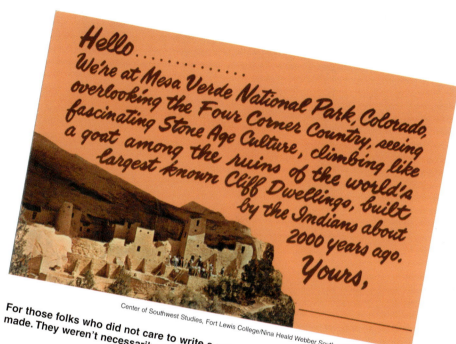

Center of Southwest Studies, Fort Lewis College/Nina Heald Webber Southwest Colorado Collection

For those folks who did not care to write a note, some postcards came ready-made. They weren't necessarily accurate, however!!

6

Founding of the Mesa Verde Company

By William C. Winkler
with Merrie Hall Winkler

Ansel Hall

The Hall family in front of their first Mancos home on Grand Avenue.

Mesa Verde Company was formed in 1937 by a group of personal friends led by Ansel F. Hall to take over concessions from the D& RG Railroad. Together with his wife June, and often aided by their six children, Ansel spent 25 years as Mesa Verde's innkeeper.

Ansel Hall had been an employee of the park service, but resigned when he was ordered to move to Washington D.C. He and his wife didn't want to raise their children in the city. It was a difficult decision.

Ansel's career had been meteoric. He was the first chief naturalist and first chief forester for the National Park Service. He established the first museum in Yosemite National Park with private funds he raised, and then went on to build more museums in other western national parks. He established the Educational Division, the Photographic Division and several other lasting interpretive facilities in the parks.

A World War I veteran, Ansel was president of the American Association of Museums and did research for them in Europe. He was a member of the Explorers Club and frequently lectured around the U.S. Both he and his wife were graduates of the University of California at Berkeley, where he served as professor of forestry for a short time. In Europe he was called on to assess war damage to the Argonne Forest. Closer to home, he was a pioneer in Oakland's East Bay Regional Park District.

Ansel's last work for the park service was with the five-year Rainbow Bridge/Monument Valley Expedition, a scientific, multidisciplinary exploration of a previously uncharted part of the U.S. Armed with 20 years' experience in all the western national parks, Ansel was not the "usual" concessioner when he took over Mesa Verde operations. In a park where the superintendent generally was "king," it made for some interesting years.

During his years at Monument Valley, Ansel became friends with John and Louisa Wade Wetherill, often staying at their home there. The couple taught him many things about Mesa Verde and about trading with the Navajo. The Wetherill family had been Mesa Verde's first concessioners, albeit unofficial ones, in the years before it became a national park. Their Alamo Ranch became the first guest lodge, and they were the original guides for visitors to the region's fabled cliff dwellings.

Ansel was no stranger to the supply side of caring for visitors. He had been a waiter at Camp Curry in Yosemite during his high school years. He was the "father" of "cooperating associations" in national parks, had written several interpretive books and encouraged artists and authors to produce art and interpretive materials in the parks. His museum building in the western national parks fostered close cooperation with those concessioners.

From its first year, with sales of slightly more than $31,000, the Mesa Verde Company grew into a business that employed 150 people and produced more than a half million dollars in revenues. In 1937 Spruce Tree Lodge could accommodate 125 visitors, primarily in tents. There were no rooms with bath. In fact, two bath tubs served guests and the entire staff. By 1962, when Ansel died, the company provided lodging for 350 guests.

It was a slow start. In its first three years the company accumulated a $12,000 deficit. Two good years had built a small surplus when disaster struck. The nation was plunged into World War II. Gasoline, tires, sugar and other essential commodities were tightly rationed. Travel ground to a halt, yet the National Park Service insisted that Mesa Verde Company maintain operations. The Halls and their children covered all bases and survived the war, but were $32,000 in debt by its end.

In 1937 the first order of business was to improve existing facilities. The lodge dining room, kitchen, lobby, and gift shop were first. Then came a program of adding bathrooms to some of the cabins. Furnishings were improved and Navajo rugs were used on the floors. Cabin 5, with its incredible view down Spruce Canyon, became the "Honeymoon Cabin." An additional bath house and toilet rooms were added for those guests and employees living in tents.

A Berkeley, California, architect was hired to design a new Spruce Tree Lodge, using the same style as the museum and superintendent's residence. The park service rejected the plan because "it could be seen from the bottom of the canyon."

Meanwhile, they developed a "Plaza Area" in the center of the Headquarters Loop and opposite the new park campground, with 39 "Deluxe Cabins." Built in a rustic duplex style, they featured knotty pine

Ansel Hall

The interior of a Plaza Area Cabin, at Spruce Tree Lodge.

milled at the nearby McPhee Lumber Mill, toilets, shower baths, and lavatories with plenty of hot water. Navajo rugs were used liberally and a few cabins even had small kitchens and dining areas. Some of the cabins were later moved out of the park and still can be seen around Montezuma County today.

For the first four years, the Hall family stayed in their Berkeley home during the winter months, then migrated to Mesa Verde each spring. In 1941, due to the war, they moved to Mancos for the "duration." After a few months Ansel took up residence in the Bauer House, which he renovated into a charming three-story home for his family of eight.

Mancos was the portal to Mesa Verde from the very beginning. It was the first park headquarters. It was the railroad terminal, the livery/stage facility, the bank, the post office, and the supply center. Logically, it became the headquarters for the Mesa Verde Company.

Ansel looked for a work space which would accommodate his new company, settling on a large commercial building at the corner of Main and Grand avenues in Mancos. The building contained 4,000 square feet of refrigeration and freezer space, a butcher shop, warehouse and workshop. It proved to be an ideal building and served as headquarters for the Aramark-Mesa Verde Company until 2005.

Ansel, in the meantime, also acquired a ranch on the Mancos River east of town, envisioning a farm where vegetables, fruits, and livestock could be raised for Spruce Tree Lodge. Leftover food scraps from the lodge could be

Fran Hall

Explorers learn how to pan for gold on the La Plata River near the Gold King Mine and Mill.

recycled as food for pigs, and a bull named "Bonanza" was bought to sire future quality beef for the tables of Spruce Tree. Unfortunately this venture did not succeed. Timing was bad, when the advent of World War II killed travel to Mesa Verde, and Ansel was forced to sell the ranch to keep his company afloat financially.

Those quiet war years gave Ansel time to plan for after the conflict when travel hopefully would resume. Prior to acquiring the Mesa Verde contract, he had organized and directed the Rainbow Bridge/Monument Valley Expedition. Before that he directed Explorer Scouts in the national parks as a part of NPS interpretation. He had also organized expeditions to Costa Rica and other exotic locations. The skills he had gained led him to create "Explorers Camp For Boys."

Ansel purchased the Gold King Mine and Mill in La Plata Canyon to serve as the base camp for operations. It had a house, assay office, and other facilities that would serve as dormitories. Local miners could teach the boys about Colorado's great mining past. Ansel hired Kenneth Ross, who had been chief of interpretation in Mesa Verde, to direct the field activities. College professors were employed to direct education in the field. As with so many other ventures, Ansel Hall was ahead of his time. He was also a pioneer in outdoor education two decades before the establishment of the National Outdoor Leadership School or Outward Bound.

Ansel planned four field camps in addition to the base camp at Gold King. One of the camps was west of Cahone, Colorado, a 46-acre Ancient Pueblo ruin purchased by Ansel. The archaeological investigations were directed by Dr. Arthur Woodard from the Museum of Man at Los Angeles,

Ansel F. Hall

The Hall family in 1945, from left: Merrie, Sylvia, Laurel, Ansel, June, Robin, Roger and Knowles. This, their second home in Mancos, was the Bauer House on North Main.

California, assisted by two archaeology graduate students from the University of Utah. This important ruin is now listed on the National Register of Historic Sites as Ansel Hall Pueblo and is part of Canyons of the Ancients National Monument. Other field camps were on the Navajo Reservation, in southeastern Utah (in part of what later became Canyonlands National Monument), Bear Creek and the western La Plata Mountains, and naturally around Mesa Verde. All of these activities provided a stimulating experience for 13-year-old Roger Hall, Ansel's youngest son. Ansel promoted the program in lectures in New York, Chicago, San Francisco, and Los Angeles. Sons were recruited from America's most culturally aware families. Some very talented young men participated, before going on to distinguished careers. They all became ardent salesmen for Mesa Verde.

An old cliché states that "behind every successful man, there is a successful woman" and this was certainly the case in the Hall household. June Alexander Hall was born in San Francisco, lived through the disastrous earthquake, and graduated with honors from the University of California at Berkeley. During the years she worked for Associated Charities in San Francisco and sang in that city's Opera Chorus, she and Ansel became acquainted. When the National Park Service sent him to Europe after World War I, she joined him in France where the couple were married.

June and Ansel built a beautiful Mediterranean home on the hill above the university and had six children, including a set of triplets. She accom-

Ansel F. Hall

June Hall pioneered the handcrafts in the Spruce Tree Lodge. She developed craft demonstrations in the park.

panied her husband on many of his trips into the western national parks, and knew park operations and park policy as well as any NPS employee. They were really a "dynamic duo." Her courage in leaving all this behind to live in a tent and do laundry in a tub in Mesa Verde is a testimony to her strength. She worked in every phase of the business, and became an expert in southwestern Native American arts and crafts. Her gift shop gained a great reputation for quality and authenticity.

After the family's move to Mancos, five of the six children – Merrie, Sylvia, Roger, Laurel and Robin – attended Wasatch Academy, a Presbyterian boarding school in Utah. The oldest son, Knowles, had elected to stay with friends in the Bay region to finish his schooling.

I had visited Mesa Verde for the first time in 1945, surveying chukkar partridges and merriam turkeys for the Colorado Game and Fish Department. Being a wildlife technician for the summer was an ideal introduction to the park. Both birds had been reintroduced into the area, and my job was to help to determine whether it was a success.

I returned to my forestry studies at Colorado A & M in 1945-46, but by the end of that year was in need of a summer job again. I responded to a newspaper "help wanted" ad for a carpenter helper, and was interviewed in Denver by June Hall. She hired me and two young men from the University of Colorado, and drove all three of us to Mesa Verde, together with her college daughter Merrie. Little did I realize I was traveling with my future wife and mother-in-law on that journey to a summer job!

Campfire Circle and the Evening Programs

The evening campfire has always been a social opportunity to meet and talk. In Mesa Verde it surely dates back to Ancestral Pueblo times. The Wetherills, Jesse Fewkes, and the first visitors brought into the park by C.B. Kelley all must have used this relaxing time of day to tell stories.

In the 1930s, the Civilian Conservation Corps built an amphitheatre using very large cut stones. It was placed in a natural cirque just north of Spruce Tree Lodge, overlooking Spruce Canyon. Now one of the park's historic structures, it is preserved, although lightly used, today. Right after World War II, the programs were in full swing and stayed active until Spruce Tree Lodge was closed.

Chief Park Naturalist Don Watson and Jean Pinkley spearheaded the evening programs in the late 1940s, always talking about some phase of Pueblo life or exploration. Each summer evening, just as the sun set, they started a campfire.

As the ranger's talk concluded, out of the darkness a dance rattle signaled the approach of a Navajo dance team. Single file, they entered the circle and Watson or Pinkley would introduce the dancers, telling about the Navajos' performances of *Yei-bi-chai*, squaw dance and round dance. Their only instrument was a small drum, enough to accompany their voices in these historic rituals.

The fire was replenished as the dances ended. Then Pack and Saddle concessioner Emmett Koppenhafer rode in. He invited visitors to join him the following day for a saddle trip, perhaps to some remote ruins in the south end of Mesa Verde. Koppenhafer was a romantic-looking man who might have stepped out of a western movie. His quick wit assured visitors of a great experience, and importantly this man knew horses and people. He quietly assured everyone, "You should not shrink from the trip because we have all kinds of horses. We have experienced horses for experienced riders. We have quiet horses for people who like a gentle ride, and for those people who have never ridden before, we have horses who have never been ridden before."

In the late 1960s, Superintendent Ron Switzer discontinued the Navajo dance programs. He reasoned that since Mesa Verde was an Ancestral Pueblo area, it was inappropriate to have Navajos performing.

That summer of 1946 began a career in Mesa Verde for me that would span 36 years and beyond, interrupted only by college studies and seasonal work for the National Park Service. Merrie and I were married in 1949 and the team we built has lasted 56 years, cheered on by our five children.

Getting around wasn't easy in those early days of my career. In the mid-1940s, it was necessary to take a train or car to obtain supplies, recruit employees, advertise, and promote the company through lectures. June once used a red dinner napkin to flag down the train to put a load of laundry from Spruce Tree Lodge on board. Mancos was well served for freight and passengers, although passengers often had to stay over on a trip to Denver. The narrow gauge railroad ran to Alamosa, where passengers were obliged to transfer to a standard gauge for the rest of the trip.

At an early point in park operations no one would deliver into the park. The Halls had to haul everything, even the laundry. After a deep well was drilled, the water from it was so hard and alkaline that washing white linen was impossible. They had to buy more linens and make one or two trips a week to a laundry in Durango. The truck would leave the park at 5 a.m. and drive to Durango to get the linens in early. Banking came next, making deposits and picking up change. Then the driver would proceed to Durango Mercantile to order wholesale groceries for the week. After picking up an order at the soft drink bottling works, the driver would begin loading the groceries and at 5 p.m. pick up the clean, ironed and packaged linens. After picking up any employees who had come to town on their day off, the heavily loaded truck would travel west up the winding Wildcat Creek road alongside the Rio Grande Southern tracks to Hesperus and then on to Mesa Verde. Arrival was always late, and the truck had to be unloaded when it arrived.

Ansel handled the load personally until 1946 when I arrived on the scene. A strong friendship developed between us. Ansel liked the fact that I was earning my way through forestry school in college and had lots of mechanical skills to boot. I admired Ansel, and found him both easy to follow and a dynamic icon for the National Park Service. He would say, "You cannot be a good concessioner, until you fully understand what the park service is."

While still a member of the National Park Service, Ansel had been enthusiastic about a "Southern Scenic Circle of National Parks" which would tie Four Corners parks together with one easy roadway. Years later, the route was strongly promoted as "The Grand Circle." Ansel's promotional skills were something to be envied. His vast knowledge and experience in the western states made him a leader among travel advocates. Free from the responsibilities of the national parks, he could concentrate on Mesa Verde and how to improve awareness and travel to this area.

In 1938 he had used the scenic route concept to develop "A Plan for Marking the Scenic Highways through the Southern Rockies."

William Winkler

The Governors of Four Corners meet in 1949 to have lunch, each sitting in his own state. Colorado Governor William Lee Knous is second from right.

Montezuma County Commissioners and Colorado Representative Betty Pellet helped secure Works Progress Administration funds to pay for the project. As an incentive, Mesa Verde Company paid for, constructed and installed the first four signs. They bought land at the intersection of highways 160 and 550, five miles south of Durango for one of the signs.

Ansel had bigger plans for the highways. Working through the chambers of commerce in Durango and Cortez, he enlisted a group of men and women to form The Navajo Trail Association. Their goal was to extend U.S. Highway 160 westward through the Navajo Reservation to Flagstaff, Arizona, and eastward to Walsenburg, Colorado, then on to Garden City, Kansas. This new highway link would save 175 miles on the route from Los Angeles to Chicago. Ansel was appointed executive director of the new association and worked tirelessly for more than 20 years to see the project come into the federal highway system.

Ansel's promotional efforts alone could fill a book. On one occasion he had a road bulldozed from Bechlabito, on the Navajo Reservation south of the Four Corners, several miles up to the exact spot of the corners. The governors of all four states were invited to a ceremony initiating the construction project and all attended. Thousands of people watched as the governors had lunch on a card table set over the exact spot, with each governor sitting in his own state. Box lunches had been prepared in the kitchen of Spruce Tree Lodge. The lodge also provided snacks to the public, and beverages were donated by Dave McGraw and Jackson Clark of Durango.

Each governor received a large album with photos of the Four Corners

TOURS AND TRANSPORTATION

The ruins in Mesa Verde are spread out in several canyons and on the mesa tops. Visitors arriving by public transportation needed help getting to the ruins beyond the Spruce Tree Area. The best interpretive experiences were those with a trained guide who could explain the many periods of Ancestral Puebloan occupation. In the very earliest years tours were conducted on horseback. "Saddle Lectures" continued through the Emmett Koppenhafer years.

Once there were roads on Chapin Mesa leading to Cliff Palace, Balcony House, and later, the mesa top structures, the park service offered organized auto caravan tours. Chief Park Naturalist Don Watson developed the auto caravan into an art form. He seized the opportunity to explain more than the cultural history, adding natural history and conservation as important elements.

On one such tour, everyone unloaded and followed their guide to the ruin, then returned to the cars following the lecture. One man sat in his car, calmly peeling an orange and throwing each piece of peel out the window. Watson watched him for a moment, then bent over, carefully picked up all the orange peels and calmly dropped them back through the window into the man's lap.

Mesa Verde Company would provide a car and driver for visitors who came into the park on public transportation. Taking them on the caravan tours, the drivers listened to the repeated lectures and soon became skilled in the answers. Since Ansel Hall had played a major role in NPS interpretation, it was only natural that all lodge employees be knowledgeable and be able to answer visitor questions. Interpretation was not an 8-to-5 situation in his lodge.

At first the Mesa Verde Company used Ford "Woody" station wagons. When more seating was needed, Ansel called on a friend in California who dealt in government surplus vehicles. For the tours he found "stretch" limos made during the war by cutting a Chevrolet sedan in two, welding a section in between and presto, seating for 12! Two of these vehicles served until the late 1950s. Later, a used motor coach was put into service.

Ansel F. Hall

Mesa Verde Company's first vehicles were purchased from the Rainbow Bridge/Monument Valley Expedition.

Auto caravans lasted into the 1950s when the number of visitors increased so much that the park was forced to change to self-guided tours.

parks and monuments, plus Monument Valley, which would now become more accessible. The beautiful leather-bound albums were prepared in the studios of Mesa Verde Company, using photos taken by Ansel.

A master of "networking" long before this notion became popular, Ansel maintained memberships in many chambers of commerce including Gallup, Grand Junction, Flagstaff and Walsenburg. He was an early member of Western Colorado's Club-20 and the Denver Convention and Visitor Bureau. Daggett Harvey and Joe Ernst of Grand Canyon were personal friends, and he stayed in Harvey Houses often. In fact Ansel was friends with all of the western national park concessioners, visiting with them frequently to discuss their common operating problems. Out of those contacts grew the Conference of National Park Concessioners.

The Mesa Verde Company's prime promotional tool was the Mesa Verde Map & Guide, a brochure that was folded to rack card size. The front panel featured a picture of Cliff Palace and inside was vital information on how to get to Mesa Verde, all the services in the park, and finally a "cartoon style" map.

Every spring Ansel would load a station wagon with the brochures and head out "to pound the drums," usually the first week of May and again right after Labor Day. He covered every chamber of commerce, motel, restaurant, and the many gas stations in a 500-mile radius of Mesa Verde. It was a lot of travel and a lot of work, but worthwhile.

He would pop through the door and say, "Here are your new Mesa Verde Map & Guides. Tell everyone that we are open and rooms are available." Then he would add the clincher – he gave most of them a business card which read, "This card is good for a free room at Spruce Tree Lodge from May 1 through June 5 and again from September 7 thru October 15." The brochures, card and personal contact really produced results and were continued through the 1970s. Eventually we obtained a printing press and printed many more thousands of the brochures during the quiet winter months in Mancos.

Finally, the program was so successful, we converted to having full color brochures printed in Chicago, hundreds of thousands of them. Merrie was grateful they came folded. Her dad had made all the kids fold brochures to save money. It was time to have them delivered by a company in the business of maintaining racks year-round. The program lost some of its edge because the message was not the same as Ansel's. Many years later old-time business people would ask me, "What ever happened to that old fellow that ran the park? He always invited me to come up and be his guest, but I never could."

7

Old Problems, New Problems
1940s-1970s

By Duane A. Smith

The year World War II ended, 1945, marked an upturn in Mesa Verde attendance to nearly 13,000. Gas rationing eventually ended, new cars again appeared in dealers' showrooms, the American economy revived from the depression '30s, and a collective wanderlust settled over the land. Americans' love affair with their automobiles and national parks had never been stronger and visitors started to arrive in record numbers. Within seven years, Mesa Verde topped 100,000 visitors and by 1958, 200,000 per year. That number nearly equaled the total that had come to the park in the first 30 years of its history.

This mass migration arrived at all national parks in unprecedented numbers. Arthur Gomez, writing in his book *The Golden Circle,* observed "visitations to the nation's parks and recreation areas jumped to an all-time high of more than twenty-one million people scarcely one year after the surrender of Germany and Japan." This created problems of overcrowding, under-funding, traffic congestion, insufficient staffing, and inadequate services. In Mesa Verde's case, its popularity particularly endangered the fragile ruins themselves with unprecedented crowd pressures. Adding this together, it totally threatened the quality of the tourists' experience.

> "COLORADANS ALMOST EVERYWHERE LOOKED WITH GOLDEN EXPECTATIONS AT THEIR TWO NATIONAL PARKS AND EIGHT NATIONAL MONUMENTS, TOGETHER WITH ALL THE NATIONAL FORESTS."

Local communities, nearly beside themselves with joy while contemplating this sudden bonanza, worried little about such matters. Never had tourism been so promising and so very definitely needed. The base economy had shifted from declining agriculture and mining to oil and gas exploration and development and expanding tourism. Coloradans almost everywhere looked with golden expectations at their two national parks and eight national monuments, together with all the national forests. The state tied for second among all the states for the highest total of Uncle Sam's lands.

For Mesa Verde, the essentials had almost all fallen into place. While needing improvement, the crucial road systems – east, north, and south – were in place and would soon be modernized. More restaurants, motels, and gas stations than ever before stood ready to accommodate the traveling public's requirements. Local communities eagerly awaited the oncoming tourists, and the park offered better facilities to handle visitors. Tried and true methods of publicity were ready to lure them into the Four Corners

Center of Southwest Studies, Fort Lewis College

Fake "cliff dwellings" at Manitou Springs.

region. Mesa Verde even undertook a new approach to promotion, a float in Durango's Spanish Trails Fiesta which the superintendent deemed "very well received" by the viewers.

As the postwar era dawned, a few storm clouds shaded the horizon. Virginia McClurg's fake Manitou Springs cliff dwellings continued to haunt Mesa Verde as they had for nearly three decades. Upset with her failure to control the park, McClurg had spitefully helped create the phony cliff dwellings. Mesa Verde Superintendent Robert Rose noted, in a July 1946 staff meeting, that a number of visitors complained that Manitou Springs had told them falsehoods about the "fake Mesa Verde Cliff dwellings" whose ruins, they claimed, could not compare with Manitou Springs. They had been told that visitors had to ride horses "many miles over poor trails, without guides" even to reach ruins at the park!

This problem had festered ever since Virginia stomped off in a huff. The park service had tried for years to correct the misinformation, but accomplished little except to force them to stop false published advertising. Observed Rose "their oral advertising continues as unscrupulous as ever. Of course, persons who subsequently come to Mesa Verde 'see the light'." Such brazen misrepresentation continued for years, and would not easily go away. Fortunately, the traveling public eventually gained a better understanding about Mesa Verde and thereafter proved less easily bamboozled.

Exactly as before the war, and during it as well, roads continued to take up a great deal of time, discussion, and concern inside and outside the park. Officials had for years worried, written, and worked on them and yet it seemed that road problems never went away for long. "However it is not in error to say that road construction or major maintenance has continued to some degree from June 1911 to today, 36 years of struggle with unstable foundations and ever improving road standards," noted assistant superintendent Ward Yeager.

Not only Mesa Verde worried about roads. The Cortez Chamber of Commerce, for instance, pushed to have Route 666 oiled and when it was not done in a timely fashion looked around for a culprit. In its eyes, it found one, Aztec, New Mexico. Wrote the Chamber's secretary, "I know positively that Aztec has a little finger in the deal." If they hoped to funnel the touring public through Aztec, their hope quickly faded. The improvement of Highway 666, realigned, resurfaced and oiled from Gallup to Cortez, ended that dream.

Improved roads encouraged another development, better signs about Mesa Verde along Highway 666. Jesse Nusbaum, who served as acting superintendent during the war, commented in a September 1945 letter that visitors had "long complained" about the lack of proper information and directional signs. Neither the park nor the Cortez Chamber of Commerce, he added, "deemed it advisable to encourage tourist travel over this seriously deteriorated and seldom maintained New Mexico section" from Shiprock northward. Now with the highway improved, he wanted signs directing people to the park.

Attention also focused on improving Wolf Creek Pass. As the Salida Chamber of Commerce complained, "thousands of people have avoided 'the closest State to Heaven' because of the condition of Wolf Creek Pass." That might have exaggerated the fear, yet the pass' reputation had not improved over the years. Narrow and steep, it had only barely improved over the days when turnouts allowed cars to pass.

Denver, too, complained about the pass, the only unpaved part of the road from Denver to Durango. Oiling that stretch would be the first step. Because of damage to tires caused by the road conditions, some drivers hesitated to cross Wolf Creek. Oiling it would, at least, help ease that worry. Unfortunately, the Colorado Highway Department proved somewhat of a road block. Because of the pass' high elevation, 10,850 feet, summer rainfall kept it from being "dusty or disagreeable" and keeping it open in the winter would not be feasible. Therefore, the department argued that it "can not afford to take the chance of oiling Wolf Creek Pass, as it is our opinion the Pass could not be kept open with the kind of equipment that is used on oil roads." The heavy tractors and bulldozers utilized for snow removal, they asserted, would tear up the oiled surface.

Durango and Gallup irritated one another into a little spat over Wolf Creek Pass. The Gallup Chamber of Commerce wanted to know the condition of the pass in order to tell travelers, and offered to pay the expense of Durango telephoning or telegraphing road conditions. When Durango did nothing, they did not "restate our offer." Durango, on the other hand, questioned why they should help Gallup.

Such teapot tempests, and even the highway improvements that occurred, paled in comparison to what was about to happen to the region. Peace did not come to the world in 1945 despite the end of the war. The Soviet Union, using communism as its cover, expanded an empire into eastern Europe and fomented communist revolutions in other areas. The United States rose to meet the challenge and the Cold War launched its generation of troubles.

Militarily, the ultimate weapon emerged, the atomic bomb. Dropping two of them on Japan had taken that country out of the war in August

1945 and, at the moment, the United States controlled a monopoly of this weapon. How did this relate to Mesa Verde National Park and its neighboring four states? "Elementary," as Sherlock Holmes exclaimed. The region contained strategic deposits of pitchblende and carnotite which when refined produced uranium for the bomb and also vanadium, which was vital for manufacturing steel among other uses.

The federal government in 1942 reopened Durango's closed gold and silver smelter as a uranium mill. Some of the ore used in atomic bombs was processed at the mill. The mill closed at the end of the war, then reopened in 1947 as the Cold War intensified. When the Soviet Union gained the bomb, and then the Korean War broke out in 1950, the urgency increased. Transportation of ore from isolated mines in the Four Corners states to the mill had always been difficult because of the poor road system through this part of the southwestern region, especially beyond the main highway from Durango to Cortez.

Back in the 1930s, as a possible world war neared, the federal government realized the need for a better national road system. Improvements started under the Defense Highway Act of 1941 and eventually benefits came to the Four Corners states. That act authorized construction, maintenance and improvement funds for roads "deemed necessary" to the war effort or "important in safeguarding the nation against enemy attack." This included interstate highways and secondary roads for which the federal government paid 75% of construction costs. The 1944 Federal Highway Act broadened the idea to include both military and civilian highway requirements. The government further expanded this plan with the Federal Aid Highway Act of 1950 that set aside money for road building on federal lands, Indian reservations, and, of particular interest, national parks. All three of these acts potentially could benefit Mesa Verde and tourism.

The uranium excitement that hit the area in the late 1940s and 1950s dramatically increased the need for improved roads. Where once the railroad had provided the economic and transportation links between isolated communities and over wide expanses, now cars and trucks had surged to replace them. Once more Uncle Sam stepped into the breach to provide funds. The Atomic Energy Commission, the AEC, oversaw the mining and milling as well as the designation of needed transportation arteries. The combination of the Cold War, Korean War, and the AEC ignited unparalleled regional highway improvements.

That rugged canyon country of the Four Corners, the AEC argued, demanded massive federal assistance in the access program to transport strategic uranium ore to the mill. "The largest section of the country in which there are no improved roads, now furnishes a large part of the domestic supply of uranium ore," declared AEC officials.

The result became obvious almost immediately. Highway 160 between Durango and Cortez and beyond into uranium rich southeastern Utah and

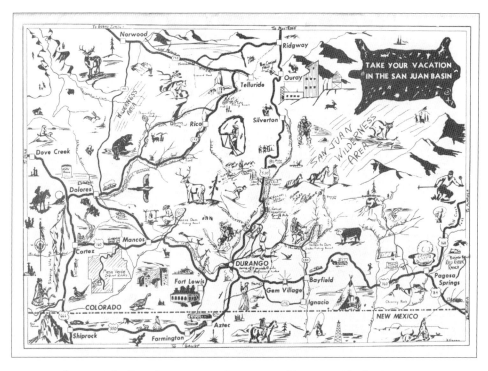

A map of the Four Corners area that appeared in a pamphlet in the 1950s.

northeastern Arizona was improved and modernized. The route was even shortened between the two towns. While Washington intended those improvements for ore transport trucks, government vehicles and prospectors, they also benefitted tourists.

Eventually Highway 160 east from Durango was upgraded as well. The paving of Wolf Creek Pass finally came about and in an ongoing project over the next generation widened and improved the highway until it became one of the best and prettiest of Colorado's mountain passes. Locals did not, however, realize all of their expectations. Despite pleas about national defense, neither Durangoans nor anyone else ever managed to interest the government in, or succeed in attaining, an interstate highway through the Four Corners. They missed on all sides as the interstates ran far to the north and south through larger population areas.

Finally, however, the construction of a paved road from Farmington (1950) replaced the primitive one in use for generations. That came about as much because of the needs of the booming San Juan Basin oil fields and the oil industry as it did in response to demands for better roads to accommodate uranium mining requirements. The improved road tied another major city into Mesa Verde, leaving only a western access unimproved.

Nevertheless, the AEC did most of the regional road construction resulting in, from 1951-55, some 800 miles of roads built in the Four

Corners states. This included building or upgrading roads across the Navajo Reservation that finally hitched Flagstaff into Mesa Verde's orbit. Californians and Arizonans could now arrive more directly and quickly than ever before.

The Federal Highway Act of 1956 followed, establishing the national interstate and "defense" highway system. Even though they did not come to the Four Corners, the interstates benefited the region. I-70 ran through Grand Junction to the north, I-25 through Santa Fe and Albuquerque, and I-40 through Gallup and Flagstaff. From these interstates, roads built by the AEC, then improved and maintained with state and federal money brought visitors to Mesa Verde with an ease and speed that had been unimaginable a generation before.

All this did not happen without some urban jealousy. The chambers of commerce in Cortez and Durango requested a road, the Navajo Trail, that would connect them to the Grand Canyon. Farmington, Moab, and their local county commissioners objected because it bypassed them. Flagstaff leaders feared such a route, as well, favoring Highway 66 as the most direct, all-winter, route. Their worry about possible loss of tourism and business appeared shortsighted as a route across the Navajo Reservation would benefit them even more than the roundabout highway they backed. Mesa Verde officials tried to stay well away from such arguments, believing the more roads the better.

Intercity bickering aside, this road building effort significantly improved park tourism. All these highways tied Mesa Verde into the thriving tourist market in Southern California and Arizona and east to Texas. No area in the country was growing faster at the time. It also became easier, if only slightly quicker, to drive from Denver and its booming suburbs to southwestern Colorado. The results proved striking and produced some old problems at unprecedented levels. During the 1963 season, 325,306 tourists arrived and four years later the park broke the seasonal 500,000 mark.

Meanwhile, another obstacle remained, the narrow, scary Knife Edge road. Some tourists became so panicked at the thought of driving over it that they did not come. Those who did told others about their harrowing experience. Not all who had driven into the park wanted to repeat the experience, a major impediment to going home! Off-duty rangers, or someone else, had to drive their cars across Knife Edge. Almost all park employees had their Knife Edge stories. One from 1948 recounted that a long string of cars was moving very slowly in reaction to the sight of a terrified man and woman slowly crawling along in the gutter feeling their way against the cliff face. "Between them and the right-hand side of the road, another person was driving their car." Until this skinny, frightening "cliffside" stretch was removed, the drive into Mesa Verde caused stress and hesitation for a number of individuals.

Mesa Verde National Park

Knife Edge slide, November 1941.

To make matters worse, slides also frequently covered one or another part of this road and sections of it sometimes slipped downhill toward the valley a thousand feet below. That never encouraged the faint of heart or fostered confidence among timid or adventuresome but inexperienced drivers. The solution required rerouting the road on the east side of Point Lookout and then westward to intersect the road beyond Knife Edge. When finally completed in 1957, the new route included a quarter-mile tunnel, then the longest car tunnel in Colorado. The road, the *Denver Post* (September 16) proclaimed, made a shorter and safer route to Chapin Mesa and eliminated "the hair-raising 'knife-edge' road so notorious among tourists."

For a while in the 1940s and 1950s, the development of the region's natural resources – oil, uranium, natural gas – seemed to overshadow tourism. Indeed, the impact of this startled folks and generated prosperity unknown for decades. Durango's 1960 population nearly doubled over that of 20 years earlier, to 10,530. Farmington, which had been smaller than its neighbor, beat that increase easily. Now the community emerged as the region's largest with 27,300 residents. Cortez, which initially benefited more from uranium than oil and gas, entered the 1960s with nearly a sixfold increase, reaching a population of 6,784 by 1960.

1950s promotional pamphlet promoting Durango and the surrounding area.

Such developments might have temporarily gained dominance, but they would not be permanent. Energy resources have a way of becoming depleted, or no longer as valuable. Tourism hopefully would continue to grow. Durangoans never gave up on championing tourism, touting their community as the "vacation capital of the West." Mesa Verde represented only part of their package. They also expected that skiing, the historic narrow gauge train trip to Silverton, the San Juan National Forest, and the mountains would lure visitors to the valley of the Animas.

A promotional pamphlet, "Durango Colorado" first encouraged visitors to see Mesa Verde, "the land of wonder," suggesting this "unique" national park required at least "two days intensive sight seeing" and also offered "Indian dances, films, and lectures nightly." Twice daily bus "schedules" from Durango, the "place to start," were also available. Of course, the pamphlet stressed all the reasons one should stay even longer in Durango. While the publication encouraged people to stay for different reasons, the idea held great merit. Tourists needed those two days at Mesa Verde to gain a better understanding of that cultural site, just as they had in earlier days.

Durango, "the town with a future," still led in the number of motels (33), hotels (5) and restaurants and eating outlets (65), and broadcast its attributes through two radio stations and a daily newspaper. It also had become the home of Fort Lewis College, broadening its cultural, economic, and educational base. Despite its growth spurt, Cortez could not match its rival, although it had several restaurants, a hotel, and 14 motels to meet the needs of tourists.

Finally though, Cortez, "a focal point for tourists," seriously contended in the game of attracting Mesa Verde visitors, particularly those coming from the west. It promoted itself as being within a short driving distance of the park, the Ute Mountain Ute Reservation, and several national monuments – Hovenweep and Yucca House. Despite typical urban rivalry, chambers of commerce in Durango and Cortez promoted Mesa Verde National Park while emphasizing each being the place to "stop and stay awhile."

Durango had a further advantage because it had the best airport near Mesa Verde. Although Farmington might contest that claim, it was farther away from the park. Cortez also gained an airport, but smaller than the other two. Frontier Airlines flew to all three and, like the railroads of an earlier era, promoted Mesa Verde as a place to visit to help increase its passenger traffic. While most Americans had not yet taken to flying vacations, planes offered a speed and ease never before available in reaching the Four Corners and Mesa Verde. The park, by plane and then car, now could be reached in about three hours from Denver. Frontier's promotion also benefited the park by helping to entice visitors to come even if they did not fly Frontier to get there.

While Durango and Cortez emerged as destination points, poor Mancos had retreated to little more than a look in the rearview mirror as one traveled by. The energy boom also bypassed the community and, in truth, it had changed so little that the Wetherills might have recognized it without trouble. The new highway skirted the town and with a population of only 832, Mancos sadly no longer represented much of a factor in Mesa Verde's present or future.

Promotion continued unabated from all the nearby and regional communities. The Navajo Trail Association, with members far to the west and east along Highway 160, particularly pushed their road as that ever popular gateway to Mesa Verde. Superintendent Robert Rose thanked the association in August 1952 for its contribution to boosting park attendance. "We all appreciate your continued interest in all communities located upon, and close to, our Navajo Trail." Chambers of commerce, the park itself, radio, the concessioner (Mesa Verde Company), and individuals all boosted the park. Maps, fliers, photographs, interviews, newspaper and magazine articles, and radio shows invited folks to come. The nearer one drew to the park, the more intense became the promotion.

Another new publicity outlet made its appearance as well. The Superintendent's Monthly Report for September 1945 noted that a television photographer had been in the park to make a children's educational program. Most Americans had no idea what television was at the time and no Four Corners resident could even receive a TV signal. Within a decade or so, TV would become a powerful commercial outlet not only in America, but throughout the world and Mesa Verde would benefit immensely from it.

Did all this and the better roads work to bring newcomers? The yearly totals said yes and so did the breakdown of where visitors came from. In 1945, cars arrived from Colorado nearly five times more than any other state, with 1,378. By the end of the 1952 season, 4,080 California cars, and 3,488 from Texas easily surpassed neighboring Utah, New Mexico, and Arizona, although Colorado still led with more than 7,700.

The park they came to see steadily grew more crowded, fulfilling Jesse Nusbaum's predictions in the 1920s. It offered, however, new conveniences and tried to keep up with the changing times. The possibility of year-round operation gained new support. The season had changed slightly from earlier days to May 15-October 15. Being open all year would have the advantage of taking at least some travelers away from the high summer crush and reducing visitation to a more manageable number. Although everyone realized summer would remain the peak season, year-around operation should help alleviate traffic congestion, particularly parking in the Spruce Tree complex. Less congestion would also mean less damage to the ruins from visitors traipsing through them. On the other side, there arose worries about keeping the trails and road open and safe for winter travel, the need for a larger staff, and, obviously, extra expenses for the park service.

As a first step, winter tours were given into Spruce Tree House on an irregular basis and then only when weather permitted. This left tourists in a quandary because they never knew when tours would be available. The debate lasted until 1965 when the superintendent and park service finally decided to keep Mesa Verde open all year.

The park enthusiastically publicized the new policy in neighboring communities and scheduled two tours a day (11 and 3 o'clock) through Spruce Tree House, the only ruin open during the winter. Lodging, meals, gas, and other supplies in the park, however, were not available. The 1965 decision also gave rangers a new task, shoveling snow on the trail. Snow removal aside, the 201 people who visited that December saw Mesa Verde in its striking winter beauty. They came for a short December day with only the museum and Spruce Tree House to tour, but received a bountiful reward with their new experience in the park. Still, summer overcrowding continued and the debate over how to solve it, which had started a generation ago, continued.

The Mesa Verde Company did all it could to make visitors' stays as enjoyable as possible. The *Kansas City Times* (June 22, 1956) approved of their efforts and recommended its readers stay at the "modern overnight accommodations" while studying a "civilization of yesterday."

A potpourri of changes came to the park, all aimed at enhancing visitors' enjoyment. The company built new central restrooms, offered a public self-service laundry, remodeled the bath facilities, and added new cabins. They expanded Spruce Tree Lodge, operated a larger bus that carried more sightseers, and opened a Kids Korral child care facility. Something else new appeared, the Sipapu Bar, which was "well hidden but may be located by diligent explorers." A store and service station also greeted visitors.

The government did not loosen its grip, but regulated everything from

William Winkler

Sylvia Hall runs at the Kids Korral in the late 1950s.

the cost of meals to plans for future development. While this led to some long and trying negotiations, the company continued operating profitably throughout the '50s. Still, these developments did not seem to answer all the needs or solve the crowded conditions around Spruce Tree House. Indeed, some appeared to make it worse. By the end of the decade, plans were discussed for some major changes at Mesa Verde.

One advancement visitors appreciated was the development, at long last, of an adequate water system. As far back as the 1920s, there had been talk about bringing water into the park from the La Plata Mountains northeast of Mancos. Surveys conducted in the '30s suggested the feasibility of both supply and means to reach Mesa Verde, and Congress appropriated money for construction. The Second World War then placed the project on hold. Increased visitation, when peace returned, quickly put pressure on the limited water supply and made it even more crucial to find additional water. Finally, in 1950, the West Mancos Water Supply system was completed, carrying water from the La Plata Mountains, and became the park's main source.

The 1950s had been good times for Mesa Verde. The tensions of the Cold War receded somewhat and the Korean conflict ended. Prosperity touched most Americans, the public traveled over a steadily improving road network, and national parks beckoned as popular destinations. Mesa Verde even offered a relief, claimed one weary traveler in the *New York Times* (July 2, 1950). "After experiencing eye fatigue from gaping at peaks,

Mesa Verde in the 1950s

The late 1940s had seen significant improvements in the Spruce Tree Area, including installation of bathrooms in many cabins and enhancements to the lodge building and kitchen. The 1950s dawned with promise, and visitation grew 156% for the decade.

Ansel Hall's management skills were put to the test in the 1950s. Needing more time to manage the Mesa Verde Company, he sold the Explorers Camp for Boys. Next, he hired an operations manager for Spruce Tree Lodge, soon followed by a food and beverage manager. The need for professional accounting had grown quickly, so Ansel hired a controller, whose wife joined June Hall seasonally in the gift shop.

After working for Mesa Verde Company in 1946, I joined the National Park Service the following summer and worked for them until 1953. In some shoulder seasons, I filled in with the Mesa Verde Company crew. In 1953 I went to work for my father-in-law full-time as maintenance chief.

In 1954 Ansel and several Mesa Verde Company investors formed a separate corporation, Mesa Verde Enterprises, Inc., to acquire property outside the park. Known to locals as "Hallarville," but officially named Point Lookout, a 270-acre parcel surrounded the park entrance on the south side of Highway 160. A 46-acre parcel on the north side of the highway had contained a store, service station, café, and cabins until a recent fire. Now only the cabins were left. I was appointed manager and dispatched to first clean up the still smoldering mess, then rebuild a resort type of operation.

A new service station and garage were built, along with coffee shop and gift shop. A small apartment was included in the second story of the round tower. This attractive new building created a lot of local interest. The coffee shop provided a stopping point for families that lived in the park, visitors, regular highway workers and route men. It also proved to be a great food business training ground for me. Late in the 1950s we brought in a professional chef from Fisherman's Wharf in San Francisco. The Swiss-born chef soon attracted a large local following and business was so good that the gift shop in the round tower was soon converted to a dining room.

The center of the property was reserved for a new lodge building. Meanwhile, a temporary building served as a reservation center for Spruce Tree Lodge. Easy access from the highway allowed visitors to book their rooms from the highway before they even entered the park.

The year-round Point Lookout Lodge had natural gas from its own well, which was used to heat all buildings on the property. Water was always an expensive commodity until an oil company found an aquifer at 1260 feet. We used water from that well until the Mancos Rural Water Company brought in good water from the Mancos River.

Ansel believed the scenic ridge covered with pinyon and juniper north of Point Lookout Lodge would be a good site for a guest ranch with riding trails. The Bureau of Land Management, which owned the narrow piece of land, was

Ansel F. Hall

Ansel Hall and Amy Amdrews check in two guests at Spruce Tree Lodge.

happy to get rid of it, and sold it to Mesa Verde Enterprises for $10 an acre.

Mesa Verde Company had developed a large full-time staff to handle business, but the season was still only five months long. Finding off-season work for them led to an expansion of the Mancos warehouse into year-round headquarters. We expanded offices, a butcher shop and a kitchen and used the 4,000 square feet of freezer space to stockpile food for summer operations.

The Mancos shop was a good place to repair and refinish hotel furniture. Gift shop merchandise was brought in, priced and prepared to be sent out to the shops. The office also served as a point of contact for prospective summer employees. The Point Lookout Service Station was changed into a full garage and a full-time mechanic was hired to work on company vehicles in the winter and visitor cars during the summer.

By the late 1950s June and Ansel had put together a mature management team. With their children married or in college, they leased out their Mancos home and moved to Denver for the winter months. Ansel built an office in his East Denver home and conducted business from there.

But a problem loomed for the Mesa Verde Company. A long-term contract was badly needed to justify spending more money on facilities in Mesa Verde. The problem was not unique to Mesa Verde, but existed in almost every other national park as well. With no standard NPS concessions policy, the major concessioners in western national parks decided to meet annually and discuss their operations and problems. Could they work cooperatively with the park service to improve visitor services? Their joint efforts led to the Concessions Policy Act of 1963.

– William C. Winkler with Merrie H. Winkler

gorges, waterfalls, glaciers and other natural spectacles, there is welcome mental stimulation in studying the ruins of Mesa Verde." Two generations of archaeologists would have been pleased.

With Mesa Verde's increased popularity and visitation came a threat to that "mental stimulation" and general enjoyment. In fact, it intensified dangerously. The superintendent's monthly report of July 1965 explained why. To tour the popular Cliff Palace took patience and even increased ranger-guided tours did not help. "There were times when people were strung from the top of the in-going stairway to the top of the exit ladders, a solid mass of milling humanity." This "is a potentially dangerous one both from the standpoint of the damage to the ruins and the risk of human life from crowding and joggling in the constricted spaces and confines of a cave site." The park service already had plans afoot to relieve some of these problems.

Visitors arriving at Mesa Verde in the 1960s became beneficiaries of two projects that would eventually increase their options for tours and services in the park – the Wetherill Mesa Archaeological Project and Mission 66. The former, carried on from 1958-65, was the largest archaeological program in the park's history. It had two goals, to obtain park expansion and gather scientific information. Archaeologists excavated and cleared three cliff dwellings of debris, including Long House, the second largest in the park, and excavated eight other ruins. The sites represented all stages of Mesa Verde's cultural development.

The plan went further. Developing Wetherill Mesa for tourists would presumably take pressure off the popular and well-known sites of Spruce Tree, Balcony House, and Cliff Palace on Chapin Mesa. Visitors would now have an opportunity to travel to Wetherill Mesa and see the complete story of Mesa Verde in a relatively small area. It would be 1973, however, before that mesa opened for visitation. Lack of funds and differing opinions about how to prevent or limit damage to the fragile sites kept the project on hold. The political climate of the Vietnam War era, which focused congressional attention elsewhere and fostered anti-government sentiment, helped place the project in limbo for years.

When Wetherill Mesa finally opened in June 1973, tourists could take a mini-train to visit the mesa top sites at their own leisure or travel on it to join the guided tours of Long House. They walked to Step House and the tired and thirsty enjoyed a cool drink and a rest stop at the small concession stand near the parking lot. For the first time since Mesa Verde became a national park, a major new area was opened.

Despite exhibiting spectacular sites and providing an easy, accessible look at the total cultural development of Ancestral Puebloan people, Wetherill Mesa never captured the attention of the visiting public. Even in its best years only about 10 percent of visitors traveled there and it did not relieve the pressure on the popular sites as much as expected or hoped.

Assuredly, many reasons existed. The museum and famous ruins were located elsewhere in the park. Who wanted to go home and say they did not visit Spruce Tree House, Balcony House, or Cliff Palace? Those three sites signified Mesa Verde to the visiting public. Despite crowds, there existed an ease of access at Spruce Tree House, a museum to visit, a gift shop and cafeteria, and a freedom to choose what to do, a variety lacking elsewhere. They also could easily take the other mesa top tours from this "central" point in the park.

The drive out to Wetherill Mesa, on the other hand, took time over a long road, and for some years it could only be reached by bus tours at specified times. After climbing up the curving, park entrance road, Spruce Tree tempted most people with an easier and shorter distance to travel. The new Wetherill sites took time to gather "fans" who would tell people it was a "must" visit. In a survey conducted to pinpoint the essential places in the park that visitors had seen, Wetherill Mesa ranked near the bottom.

Another factor in Wetherill Mesa's limited appeal may have been related to the length of visitors' vacations. A 1979 survey discovered that the typical tourists had time for a walk through the museum, a self-guided tour of Spruce Tree house, and an hour or so driving the scenic tour around the mesa top with its view points. Then they hurried off to their next destination. Some actually tried to do Mesa Verde *and* Grand Canyon in one day!

Mission 66 had a much longer history in planning and discussion and involved the whole park system, not simply Mesa Verde. Back in the 1950s, it had first been discussed in response to funding shortages, increased visitation, and people traveling to parks by car who wanted new facilities adapted to their needs. These familiar Mesa Verde themes now received national attention.

The specific goals for Mesa Verde included a potpourri of projects and ideas that would benefit the tourist's experience. The idea of centralizing activities on Chapin Mesa had been fine a generation before, but now sheer numbers and traffic volume overwhelmed it. A major Mission 66 goal focused on relocating the lodge, cabins, and campground to a more suitable location to at least partially resolve the Spruce Tree House jam. This idea, however, upset some people who fondly remembered that everything had been easily concentrated within walking distance around Spruce Tree House.

In addition, the visitor service program would be updated to enhance the understanding and appreciation of Mesa Verde's "unique attractions" and more staff would be added for protection, interpretation, and maintenance. Mesa Verde's story continually evolved as new interpretations and excavations challenged older ideas. These needed to be presented in an understandable manner. Also, new ideas about preservation and stabilization needed to be implemented.

The interesting and challenging objective of this plan was that all of it

William Winkler

Morefield Village provided visitor services in a campground of 512 sites.

would be accomplished while doing "business as usual." At least that was how planners visualized the goal. Discussed in the '50s, put into operation in the '60s, Mission 66 did what it set out to do – improve the visitor's stay, enjoyment and educational experience at Mesa Verde.

The National Park Service and the Mesa Verde Company selected Navajo Hill as the place for a new service station and lodge and the upper end of Morefield Canyon for the campground. The popular campfire talks migrated to Morefield as well. Construction started at Far View, as it was named, in late 1965 and the rooms were available the next spring, followed by the restaurant a little later. The new site offered magnificent, sweeping views to the south and west and did help relieve crowding farther down south at Chapin Mesa.

Planning for opening Wetherill Mesa came with this project. In the 1970s, it was anticipated that the complex might increase visitation to Wetherill Mesa, the road to which took off just west of the lodge. Such hopes were thwarted despite the ease of access.

A new generation of visitors would not know the Chapin Mesa facilities, although "older folks" continued commenting they hated to see it go as it had been a "delightful place in earlier years." Many of the familiar build-

MISSION 66

Mesa Verde National Park had five different master plans during the Ansel Hall years. The Plan of 1937-1941, Master Plan Revision of 1950, and Master Plan Revision of 1952 represented growth by logical evolution. The fourth and fifth, "Mission 66" plans, emerged by "official action" with no prior consultation or discussion.

In January 1956 NPS Director Conrad Wirth revealed the first "Mission 66" plan for converting the park to "Exclusive Day Use." All visitor lodging, food service, and stores would be removed from the park. The basis for this decision was that archaeological sites on Chapin Mesa were too dense to allow for any new facilities.

It was quickly pointed out that an "archaeological site" could be a place where two rocks were placed together for a campfire, or a simple overnight location. The one-square-mile headquarters location, where improvements were proposed, had already been used by other structures and campgrounds.

The second "Mission 66" plan acknowledged that accommodations were needed, but said they should be moved to the north rim of the park where the ruins were not so dense. Ansel Hall vigorously resisted this move, pointing out that the north rim was 1,000 feet higher in elevation, which would shorten the season. Visitors could extend their day if they could walk to the museums, (there were two at the time), campfire circle and other visitor facilities. Two senators, a congressman, Colorado's governor and a list of knowledgeable people agreed with him.

A standoff developed, which lasted for six years until Ansel's death in 1962. Some family members believe the stress of those years contributed greatly to his fatal heart attack.

The happier side of the "Mission 66" plan was the scientific excavations on Wetherill Mesa. This was the first major, multidisciplinary excavation of Mesa Verde involving the National Geographic Society. The NGS participated in 10 percent of the cost and more importantly published articles on the progress of the program. There was a direct link between the articles and the travel trends to Mesa Verde.

A very interesting group of professionals came together in Mesa Verde and enriched the lives of all of us who lived there. Some new lifelong friendships were formed which extended way beyond Mesa Verde. New knowledge improved the interpretive skills of NPS and concession workers alike. It was a great experience!

– William C. Winkler with Merrie H. Winkler

ings soon were gone, except the hospital which was remodeled into a food service facility for the visitors to Spruce Tree House, park employees' houses, a few governmental buildings, and the museum. The superintendent's home remained where Nusbaum had planned and helped build it.

These total efforts at least partially met the persistent need to relieve crowding of cars and people at the south end of Chapin Mesa and definitely opened the area more for visitors to enjoy. The number of tourists, however, quickly caught up with these efforts and on a July day, as the summer tourist season peaked, parking and bathrooms remained at a premium.

Another part of Mission 66 appeared after the major portion of the project became history, a new visitors' center also on Navajo Hill, or Far View. Here the tourist would eventually have to stop for tickets and a timeslot to tour those two popular attractions, Balcony House and Cliff Palace. Discussion of moving the park administrative facilities to near the park entrance continued to be simply that, but the dream did not die. Should that idea become a reality, Mancos would, ironically, *almost* regain the park headquarters it had lost decades before.

Small problems never went away despite big projects. Colorado went on daylight-saving time in the mid-1960s, a seemingly harmless matter for Mesa Verde. It proved the opposite, affecting visitors and service personnel alike. The museum had to open earlier as tourists arrived earlier in the cool of the mornings. And because it remained light later into the evenings, campfire talks had to start later, stretching the staff in both directions. The park rose to the challenge and visitors hardly noticed a change, except they got back to their camp or their rooms later than usual after the talks.

As is typical, visitors were not shy about making their complaints heard and generously giving compliments when deserved. With a little bit of humor, the superintendents, for a while, kept a monthly total much like the score in a game. For instance in July 1965, one reported "compliments did not quite balance out complaints" The latter won six-to-four. He did not blame it all on his staff. Of the six complaints, three people had taken exception to park service activities or personnel and three concerned the concessioner's operations.

Complaints, if rational, needed to be resolved. Compliments could be savored and enjoyed. This 1966 visitor's comment brought joy to the park people: "I was impressed at the manner in which you people conduct this operation. I am sure that foreign visitors as well as American citizens are very proud of what is being preserved for us to look at and study."

No doubt about it. Except for crowding, the visitor's experience had improved markedly in a variety of ways since the end of World War II. From lodging to the archaeological tours and interpretation, they learned more, saw a more thorough portrayal of the ancient people and times, and, if they stayed overnight, found the accommodations the best yet. Ease of access into and through the Four Corners had improved dramatically and the new road into Mesa Verde left drivers more relaxed than ever before. Not to mention that more comfortable, faster, and air conditioned cars made it a much more soothing trip through those long miles that still had to be traveled to reach the park. The steadily increasing number of tourists – more were arriving on a single summer day than came in an entire year a generation before – reflected the popularity of Mesa Verde nationally and internationally.

There was no question that tourism had regained its hold on the Four Corners. As Gomez wrote describing the energy boom's decline in the mid-1960s, it was "tourism that offset economic disaster." Tourism had become year-round with skiing and more people taking vacations in off-summer months. All this promised exciting times for the crown jewel in Four Corners promotion, Mesa Verde National Park.

SOURCES

Books
Gomez, Arthur, *Quest for the Golden Circle* (Albuquerque: University of New Mexico Press, 1994): 128, 101-07 & 112.

_____, "The Fabulous Four Corners," Unpublished PhD Dissertation, University of New Mexico, 1987: 98, 103-06, 109-10, 117, & 122.

Smith, Duane A., *Mesa Verde National Park* (Boulder: University Press of Colorado, 2002 revised edition): chapters 9 & 10.

Wenger, Gilbert, *The Story of Mesa Verde National Park* (Denver: Mesa Verde Museum Assoc., 1980): 74.

Articles
Hayes, Alden, "The Wetherill Mesa Project," *Naturalist* (1969): 22-23.

Lister, Robert, "Archeology for Layman and Scientist at Mesa Verde," *Science* (May 3, 1968): 492-98.

Publications
Unidentified newspaper clipping, May 24, 1945, Roads Outside the Park File, Mesa Verde archives.

Cortez Sentinel, August 24, 1944.

Correspondence
Memo, Staff Meeting, July 22, 1946, Mesa Verde archives.

Murray to Nusbaum, September 28, October 24, 25, & November 14, 1944, Roads Outside the Park file, Mesa Verde archives.

Nusbaum to Government John Dempsey, August 21, 1944, Roads Outside the Park file, Mesa Verde archives.

_____, to H. Murray, November 14, 1944, Roads Outside the Park file, Mesa Verde archives.

_____, to J. Stewart, September 19, 1945, Roads Outside the Park file, Mesa Verde archives.

Robert Rose to Ralph Faxon, August 28, 1952, Mesa Verde archives.

Gil Wenger to Author, August 4, 1986.

M. Woodward to W. Foshay, June 16, 1946, Roads Outside the Park file, Mesa Verde archives.

Other
1951 Map & Guide, np, Mesa Verde archives.

Colorado Yearbook (Denver: Bradford-Robinson, 1947): 152.

Colorado Year Book 1956-58 (Denver: State of Colorado, 1956): 778, & 798.

Colorado Year Book 1962-64 (Denver: State of Colorado, 1962): 818, & 822.

Durango Colorado (Durango: NP, mid-1950s).
Knife Edge story, Staff meeting, August 30, 1948, Mesa Verde archives.
Mesa Verde: General Management Plan May 1979 (Washington: US Department of the Interior, 1979): 3.
Mission 66 records, Management File, Mesa Verde archives.
Press release 1973, Mesa Verde archives.
Staff conference, November 28, 1951, Mesa Verde archives.
Travel summaries 1945 & 1952, Mesa Verde archives.
William Winkler collection.
W. Yeager report, 1946 historic file, Mesa Verde archives.

8

The Roger Hall and William Winkler Years

By William C. Winkler
with Merrie Hall Winkler

f June and Ansel Hall's six children, two would retain close ties to Mesa Verde National Park into their adult lives – Merrie, their second-born, and Roger, one of the triplets.

Roger seemed to love Mesa Verde and everything that his father did. The two became great companions and through their teacher/parent relationship Roger learned a great deal about Mesa Verde and the Southwest.

Roger participated in all of the Explorer Camp activities. In Mesa Verde when he wasn't a bellhop, he worked wherever else was needed. After graduating with honors from Wasatch Academy in Mt. Pleasant, Utah, he entered the University of Colorado under a Naval R.O.T.C. program and graduated with a degree in civil engineering. Summer programs at sea convinced him to pursue a Navy career. His education continued with a stretch at the Harvard Business School where he earned a Master of Business Administration degree. Following graduation from CU, he married Virginia Woodman and they spent some exciting years in the South Pacific.

William Winkler

Roger Hall

In March 1962 Ansel Hall became ill and died, leaving behind a legacy of great achievements in the National Park Service and as concessioner in Mesa Verde and the Southwest. June had been very active in the business, joining her husband in nearly all big decisions. Now she called on her son to return home and take over. Roger quit his beloved Navy life, returned home and became president and general manager of the Mesa Verde Company.

With the change in leadership came some changes in management as well. I was named operations manager and we assembled a new team that worked well. Our largest hurdle was our contract with the National Park Service. We had been operating on one-year contracts for at least five years, a result of the Mission 66 program and the park service's continued insistence on moving concession facilities out of the headquarters area. Excavations at Wetherill Mesa were proceeding on schedule, which meant the park would soon be able to handle many more visitors.

The Navajo Trail, a project Ansel Hall had long worked on, opened in September 1962 with immediate results. The traveling public was quick to take advantage of this alternative to the more southerly Route 66. It was a boon to Mesa Verde, as travelers passed right by on their way from

Flagstaff, Arizona, to Chicago. In the first year after the new route opened, there was a 24 percent increase in travel to the area. By the end of 1963 Mesa Verde Company recorded its highest net profit in 27 years of operation – $ 27,512.80. Roger Hall could turn his full attention toward a new contract and the development of new facilities.

The master plan called for development of concessioner's facilities on Navajo Hill and in Morefield Canyon. Sale of the company's facilities at Spruce Tree Point was more complicated. Concessioners and the National Park Service have a unique business relationship, known as possessory interest. At their expense – and always with final design approval by the park service – concessioners build lodging, dining, and other facilities on park service land, but do not truly own them. They use the facilities under a contract with the park service. The investment of years of work and thousands of dollars can, at least in theory, yield nothing for the concessioner if the contract is not renewed. Fortunately, the National Park Service and Mesa Verde Company each had the Spruce Tree Lodge facilities appraised, and the results were fairly close.

In September 1963, Roger secured a new 20-year operating contract in which the company agreed to construct visitor facilities on Navajo Hill and in Morefield Canyon, including at least 125 rooms on Navajo Hill, and an investment of at least $1,000,000 over a five-year period. The government would pay $400,000 for the old Spruce Tree facilities and give the company three more years to operate it without rent.

Roger Hall continued many of the promotional programs that had been started by his father, although the folder distribution program became so massive that a distributor was hired. Like his father, he also became active in Cortez and Durango chambers of commerce and Club-20, eventually serving as president of the regional organization. He also continued his father's traditional role in the Conference of Western National Park Concessioners.

Roger strengthened the tie with the D&RG Railroad in Durango, leading to increased reservations. Eventually Mesa Verde Company opened a service station on railroad property at the junction of highways 550 and 160 and established a "hot line" for direct reservations in Mesa Verde. He and both his triplet sisters, Robin and Laurel, all settled in Durango.

Meanwhile, back at Mesa Verde, the Wetherill Mesa crews were well into their excavations. The name Far View Lodge was adopted for the new hotel and the food service facility was named Far View Terrace. Work began on guest rooms, a service station and offices. During the transition from one area to another, Roger had a custom kitchen built into a commercial truck trailer. Food was prepared in the Spruce Tree Lodge kitchen and hauled to Far View, where it was served hot, cafeteria style.

Roger Hall also negotiated an arrangement with an oil company to participate financially in building service stations at Far View and Morefield

William Winkler

Far View Lodge became the full service center on Navajo Hill.

Campground Village. Equipped with state-of-the-art facilities, the Morefield station even included high-ceilinged service bays to allow for work on tall RVs.

As plans developed for the 1964 season, operations management was divided into two areas. I would handle the commercial division, including grocery stores, service stations, newsstand, vending machine operations and Point Lookout food, lodging, and gift shop. I also assumed responsibility for opening the campground services area by August. Roger took charge of the hotel division, overseeing construction of the first 52 rooms at Far View.

The hotel rooms were designed so that each would have a good view from a balcony with chairs. Visitors loved the quiet evening hours with great sunsets, deer nearby and an occasional calling coyote.

In Morefield Canyon, the park service built one of their largest public campgrounds, with 512 sites beautifully arranged among the oak brush. An evening campfire amphitheatre was large enough to accommodate a couple thousand visitors. They required the "Pack and Saddle" concessioner to move to this new location and re-establish his corrals and hitch-rack. Two new trails were opened for his customers, beautiful rides but without the opportunity to view any ruins.

Morefield Village was planned to contain a supermarket, a fast food outlet, public showers, a coin-op laundry, a full-service station, firewood outlet and a ranger station. In the course of two years the complex became the second largest community, population-wise, in Montezuma County during July and August, surpassed only by Cortez.

I threw myself, heart and soul, into making Morefield Village the pride of the National Park Service. Construction money was beginning to get very tight, calling for some creativity. Store furnishings were expensive, for example. Then I learned that a fairly new store in Fort Collins, Colorado, had gone bankrupt. The bank held title to all the contents and was very eager to unload them in one parcel. I made them an offer of $6,000 and they accepted. Our gift shop cases were obtained from surplus Denver Dry Goods warehouses.

Typical of the kind of details that can make or break a business, I had to figure out a way to make coin-operated showers work. At Spruce Tree campground, the coin-operated locks were reliable but could not control how long people used the showers. On several occasions our managers watched helplessly as college groups all showered for a single coin.

New technology for self-service car washing provided a solution. A 10-cent lock would control access to the shower room, while a second coin-operated mechanism timed the showers. An entire family could use a shower room for a dime, and all the hot water they wanted for 25 cents per five minutes. The only weak part was that once inside, the guest had to turn the privacy lock on the inside of the door. Despite signs inside and outside the shower rooms, people sometimes forgot to turn the locks. The next unsuspecting guest would insert a dime, then open the door. When they asked for a refund of the dime people would sometimes say, "I really shouldn't ask for a refund because it was worth it."

We also installed a free-standing coin-operated car wash, the first in Montezuma County. It proved to be very popular with campers, and served for a number of years. Then as water became scarce, the park service requested it be removed.

The service station had two "lube bays," each with a hoist that could lift RVs. We sold a full line of tires, and were open at least 16 hours a day. Our gasoline storage was very large, and a 1,000-gallon propane plant filled bottles, RVs and vehicles that ran on propane. A wrecker truck based there provided quick service all over the park. A four-wheeled, covered wagon was stationed at Morefield to provide self-service firewood sales.

Facilities at Spruce Tree remained in use and the lodge kitchen there was producing food for both locations. We had assumed for years that people rented the canvas cottages at Spruce Tree because there were no more rooms with bath available. But now, with plenty of deluxe rooms available, people still asked for the economy tents. For many years after the canvas cottages were gone, people still asked for them. When told the cabins were gone, they expressed disappointment that their children would not have the experience of sleeping in a tent.

Earnings in 1967 were a big disappointment. Construction at Far View and Morefield had consumed all available cash and loans were difficult to

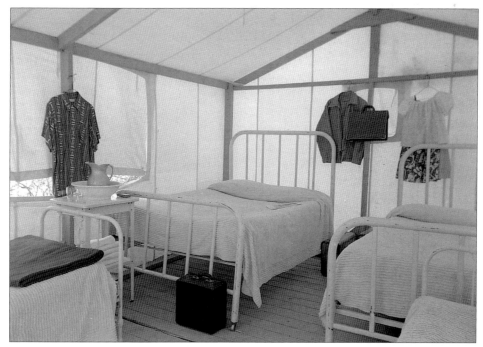

Ansel F. Hall

The interior of a canvas cottage at Spruce Tree Lodge. This 12-foot by 16-foot tent had electricity, screen windows and doors.

secure. The possessory interest arrangement with the National Park Service put the Mesa Verde Company in an unusual position compared to most businesses, with no collateral against which we could borrow for construction or improvements. Meeting during the winter of 1967-68, company directors decided administrative overhead had to be cut to the bone. Roger Hall decided to leave the company to pursue other interests. In a sad transition for everyone, I became president and general manager. Belt-tightening followed in 1968.

These were not easy years for the park service management either. There were major projects underway in Mesa Verde, with Wetherill Mesa excavations moving quickly. A vibrant group of archaeologists had been brought together along with scientists of other disciplines. There were professional people of all "stripes," plus the National Geographic Society. Then there were the roads, trail and sewer system developments, and a private contracting company utilizing union labor.

There were plenty of stressful moments to go around. To cope with them all, the National Park Service sent in Chester A. Thomas as superintendent. Thomas was an archaeologist, so coordinating the Wetherill program was second nature. He could be tough and deal with the contractor and union people equally. With the concessioner, Thomas used a great

William Winkler

Merrie and William Winkler

technique. He considered them part of his staff and invited them to all of his staff meetings. It was a great move that had never been used before, was only lightly used in the Meredith Guilett administration, and not at all after.

Working with my father-in-law had been a great learning opportunity for me. I had admired Ansel's networking ability and followed suit, joining the Cortez Lions Club. Through that club I formed a fast friendship with Superintendent Thomas. The two of us enjoyed mutual companionship in hunting and fishing, and together founded the Bauer Lake Sporting Club. The club thrived and 40 members enjoyed superior fishing from then on.

Thomas and I also worked with several other Cortez area residents to form Mesa Verde Savings and Loan Association. I served as its treasurer for 14 years, learning valuable financial lessons that served me well inside the park.

I faced a new challenge in 1968 when I was named president and general manager of the Mesa Verde Company. It helped that I had been in the "trenches" of the company for more than 20 years, and knew all the inner operations thoroughly.

We had 15 years remaining on our contract with the park service, but faced serious problems acquiring capital. All available funds had been invested in the new facilities at Far View and Morefield, but there were other major projects to be accomplished. Spruce Tree was still in service and had to be closed out.

We called together our key staff members and hatched a plan. We would tighten all expenses and make our best efforts for several years to prove to potential lenders that Mesa Verde Company was a credit-worthy account. Thanks to those efforts, the company survived.

With our five children now in school, Merrie re-entered the workplace, directing her attention to souvenirs and the growing Indian handcraft department. Buying was a year-round job and scheduling deliveries an art form that needed her attention. She set up an office in the Mancos facility and directed buying from there. Merrie continued her interior design work, which soon became a more important responsibility as the new lodging at Far View opened.

William Winkler

Merrie Winkler managed four gift shops in Mesa Verde.

Mesa Verde Company had purchased a membership in Associated Grocers of Colorado, giving us tremendous buying power, not only for food stuffs but also hotel and restaurant supplies. With the added responsibility for the hotel, I joined the Colorado/Wyoming Hotel and Motel Association and the American Hotel and Motel Association. Both offered training from the Kellogg Institute in the art of inn keeping. I soon became a vice president of the Colorado Association and held the position for many years. I also joined the American Association of Travel Agents. Analysis of room registrations showed that many guests arrived through the AAA Motor Club Reservation Service. A full page ad in their Colorado Directory resulted in increasing the house count. Ansel had taught me well about the benefits of networking.

The last year Mesa Verde Company operated Spruce Tree Lodge was, sadly, 1969. With the complete move to Far View, Far View Terrace Food finally got its own full-service kitchen. The outdoor portion of the dining space, which had been under canvas, was closed in to allow for a more complete gift shop. This was the first of several remodels to take place here. Finally we had complied with that portion of our contract which required that we leave Spruce Tree Point.

The park service soon discovered, though, that moving our facilities out of the Spruce Tree House area was a great mistake. Superintendent Meredith Guilett's desk was soon covered with complaints from the public when they discovered they had to make a slow 12-mile round trip for lunch or a roll of film. A day-use facility was badly needed at Spruce Tree. Guilett coordinated

William Winkler

Spruce Tree Terrace.

a quick plan with the regional design office and Mesa Verde Company.

Spruce Tree Terrace emerged as a temporary structure made from the vacated first aid station/hospital. We renovated the structure, preserving the beautiful Mesa Verde stone architecture, then brought in the portable kitchen we'd used to shuttle food from Spruce Tree House to Far View and attached it to the building. An outdoor deck allowed people to dine under the pinyons and junipers, while inside they could buy film and picnic supplies, browse through Native American handcrafts in the old operating room, and watch a silversmith demonstrate his skills at the front of the store.

At 1,000 feet lower than Far View, Spruce Tree Terrace has a much longer season. In fact, it became Mesa Verde Company's first full-time operation in the park and has served visitors and residents alike ever since.

A second need was quickly identified. Tauck Tour Company was bringing several large bus loads of visitors into Mesa Verde every week during the tour season. They stayed overnight at the Strater Hotel in Durango, visited the park all day and returned to the Strater each evening. They brought with them box lunches that had been prepared in the Strater kitchen and ate them in the beautiful rim-side picnic ground at Spruce Tree. With almost every visit, the trip leader came to the Mesa Verde Company cafeteria looking for something that had been left out of the box lunches.

Because tour participants ate almost all their meals in restaurants, they looked forward to lunch in this beautiful picnic ground. I suggested we could improve on the experience by providing an old-fashioned chuck wagon lunch – fresh, hot, and historically significant! Superintendent Guilett liked the idea and so the bar W chuck wagon was created.

The plans and files of the Colorado Historical Society provided a model

William Winkler

Chuck wagon located in the Spruce Tree picnic.

for an authentic set up and we had the wagon built in the Mancos workshop using an old Navajo wagon chassis. More that 6,000 lunches were served that first summer.

The early 1970s were good for business but the problem of long-term capital persisted. Banks, savings and loans, mortgage brokers, and insurance companies all gave the same reply: "Yes, you have a good earnings record, your books look great – but you don't have title to the buildings, only this thing called 'possessory interest'."

The problem finally was solved with a new explanation of Mesa Verde Company's relationship to the park service. While we didn't have title to the facilities we'd built, we had something better, the guarantee of the United States Government. We finally got the loan we needed.

Now it was time to move on to the completion of Far View Lodge and more rooms. Merrie and I spent a week traveling around the Southwest with our architect, reviewing various buildings and the things we liked about them. It was important that the flavor of the Southwest and Mesa Verde be incorporated into the new lodge's main building. We also built two new bi-level units on Far View Hill, one on each side of the main lodge, each with 20 rooms. Construction took place in one of the heaviest winters in recent times, but the rooms were opened in the summer in time to capture that critical 45-day period of peak travel. Each room had a balcony with wing walls for privacy and two deck chairs. Without the distraction of television, people turned their attention to the natural environment. They would sit on the balcony enjoying their evening beverage and watch the sun set over the mesa. Deer were plentiful around the lodge and could be seen only a few feet away. Occasionally visitors would come to

William Winkler

Far View Lodge. The main lodge served 126 rooms.

the front desk and say they'd heard a sound that sent chills up their spines. It was coyotes howling, and there were plenty of them yelping to each other over the oak-covered mesa top and into the canyons.

The main Far View Lodge was a lot of fun to create and build. It was a masonry building which could, if needed, withstand the rigors of winter at 8,000 feet elevation. Air conditioning was not needed at this elevation, but a great air movement system was engineered to keep constantly fresh air moving throughout the building without the sensation of "wind." We wanted the building to have the appearance of a Far View ruin. The masonry walls were stucco in an adobe color with the material applied as though a Pueblo person had done it by hand. One feature was a round tower with a stairwell leading up to an attractive cocktail lounge.

Merrie was involved in every detail of the new lodge building. Visitors entered through a pair of wooden raised-panel doors, stepping into a lobby that seemed to be set back in time. Floors were saltillo tile, and a planked ceiling stretched throughout this level into the dining room. The light fixtures were handmade by the famed Jemez potter Reyes Madelina, decorated by us in classic Mesa Verde black on white designs, then returned for firing. A Pueblo style fireplace stood in the corner, a writing desk and comfortable seating nearby. Navajo rugs and paintings adorned the off-white stucco walls. Adjacent to the lobby was a small Indian handcraft shop.

The dining room was a work of art and a point of great pride. Merrie and the architect had arranged the fenestration so that every table had a view through large windows. Upper and lower levels were separated by two steps, giving everyone a view. Some could look out to the La Plata Mountains over the mesa, others looked south over the mesa top to Shiprock and the Chuska and Lukachukai mountains in the Southwest. All views were great at sunset when lucky diners could even watch the occasional deer.

An unhurried management philosophy was important in the dining room. There was a good cafeteria at Far View Terrace, for those who were in a hurry or on a very limited budget. The lodge dining room could seat approximately 125 people. Two "turnovers" per evening were all that was desired. The fact that Mesa Verde National Park was set aside for the works of man meant he lived here 24 hours per day. He was not a "day-use visitor." It was important to recognize prehistoric man in this setting. The menu should reflect as nearly as possible the items that the Puebloans might have eaten.

Menu items included prime roast leg of lamb to reflect the mountain sheep of the canyons. Roast duckling glazed with special chokecherry sauce, both native to the mesa, were served. Tender young rabbit, grown especially for this kitchen, resembled the cottontail and jack rabbit that were found all over the mesa. There was a USDA choice grade sirloin steak served *carne asada* with a special chili sauce for those with less adventuresome taste. The trimmings all reflected the trinity of corn, squash, and beans.

A compote relish was served with each meal. There was corn chowder soup and a special appetizer of fried squash blossoms was available in season. These were locally-grown, and delivered to the lodge kitchen fresh daily. Individual loaves of freshly baked bread, pies and desserts rounded out the meal.

Wines, a good selection of beers, and cocktails were also available. The waiters, waitresses, and bus people all wore a pueblo style shirt with white trousers and a pouch attached to a hand-loomed sash for their meal checks.

The finishing touch to this attractive scene was a troubadour who played Mexican-style guitar music. Manuel Delgado had a beautiful baritone voice and a huge repertoire of songs. The hours of the dining room were posted as 5 p.m. until 9 p.m., but many evenings it would be almost midnight before the staff got out of the dining room.

A small cocktail lounge, the "Sipapu" (Hopi term for entrance to the spirit world), was constructed in the third level of the round tower. There was some indoor seating, with more on the patio. This lounge was never a big thing, but it did give a few visitors a place to meet and talk in the evening.

With the closure of Spruce Tree Lodge, the evening campfire programs were moved to the Morefield Amphitheatre, leaving no evening programs for lodge guests. So we set up the lower meeting room for evening programs with talks by rangers and other guests. This would have been an excellent time to show films telling the story of Mesa Verde, but none existed – a void we quickly moved to fill.

The supplier of slides and films to our gift shops wanted to produce a full-sound 16mm film on a broad scale. Mesa Verde Company agreed to pay development costs for an educational film. The film company sent two professional cameramen plus equipment and film. I directed the shoot and wrote the script and an actor provided the narration. The film was a great success and was shown nightly for many years in the meeting room of Far View Lodge.

Colorado Governor John Vanderhoof had appointed me to serve as a member of the State's Centennial/Bicentennial Commission. One special meeting was held in Mesa Verde and the governor attended with his girlfriend "Mary Lynn." After everyone had left, I took the governor and his friend on a special trip to see a Wetherill Mesa ruin. This area had been completed but not yet opened to the public. A picnic lunch was enjoyed on the rim of the canyon. John proposed to Mary Lynn on this trip and she accepted. Mary Lynn was a television personality with a daytime show on regional NBC. She loved Far View Lodge and our film and asked to show it on NBC. Naturally she got permission and showed it several times. She had scenes of the rooms and lodge televised and showed them, too, on her daytime program. What a great "infomercial."

The first full year of operating the new lodge was a good one. The staff had done a great job, so as a reward we planned a special trip for them. We packed leftover supplies into large picnic hampers along with snacks and beverages and boarded a tour bus to Grand Teton and Yellowstone National Park. The first night was spent with a great national park hotel man, Stuart Cross, now at the Hotel Utah. A great interpretive program was held there. Then it was on to Yellowstone to visit friends at Hamilton Stores and more interpretation. A grand finale was held at the Explorer's Museum at the confluence of the Madison and Fire Hole rivers. Here we heard about the beginnings of the National Park Service. It snowed that historic day and everyone felt a closer tie to the mission of the National Park Service.

Back at Mesa Verde plans were developing for a third remodel of Far View Terrace. Business was good at this location and needed expansion. The kitchen and cafeteria line were completely rebuilt, expanding into the service station repair bays, which had not been profitable. An outdoor eating plaza was built on the west side and equipped with tables and chairs. A large solar hot water heating system was cleverly installed on the west edge of the patio. A unique refrigerated, circular cafeteria counter which slowly revolved graced the center of the cafeteria. The canopy over the counter gave a back-lighted stained glass appearance with modern Pueblo pottery designs. It was beautiful.

The gift shop received a heavy treatment. The south-facing windows were closed off. A second story was added to the southwest, combined with a cov-

William Winkler

Early tour bus.

ered entrance to the cafeteria. A tiny spot for trees and grass was bounded by a low adobe wall. It contained a large multi-tiered fountain which recycled water to produce a gentle trickling sound. What a lovely spot to relax.

The remodel included a tower similar to the lodge. The upstairs was devoted to racks of Navajo rugs, hundreds of them with plenty of space to display them. A policy of lower margins and very high quality yielded many returning customers from even as far away as Europe. We sold more than 600 rugs per year, thanks to Merrie's great connections for Indian handcrafts.

Tours continued to be a very important part of Mesa Verde Company activities. The contract provided exclusive rights for commercial tours in Mesa Verde. Each spring tour guides were schooled along with the national park seasonal interpreters. In addition the company had its own training programs. Some were by in-house people, others by guest archaeologists. The company tour people were good and they were paid very well. A large number of local school teachers filled these ranks.

The Mesa Verde Company by this time owned several tour busses. Some would depart from Far View Lodge twice a day for ruins tours. Others provided regular bus service from Cortez, connecting with Continental Trailways busses. They also bussed employees from Cortez and Point Lookout twice daily. The bus business grew rapidly and the park service appreciated the boost in interpretation.

In 1976 Superintendent Ron Switzer called a meeting with me to outline the need to get Wetherill Mesa open and running. The ruins excavations had been completed and the highway there recently paved. A trail wide enough for a vehicle was paved to each of the mesa top trailheads and ruins. With the regional NPS office "bogged down" with other priorities, Switzer wanted the Mesa Verde Company to get it open with transportation.

Mesa Verde Pack & Saddle

Horses played an important role in the first 75 years of Mesa Verde tourism. They were the standard mode of transportation for the Wetherills, the first visitors to Mesa Verde and the Ute Indians. Goods were brought into the park on pack horses. C.B. Kelly maintained a stable in Mancos and had corrals at Spruce Tree headquarters.

The corrals were later moved to a convenient location in the trees above the Spruce Tree House Ruin, where a small cabin was built for the new concessioner. Lodging developed to the west on the other side of Spruce Tree Canyon, and a new campground was built to the south. Jim English provided this service into the late 1930s, assisted by Clarence "Tuffy" Teague, Jim Neeley, Jack Wade and several others. Jack Wade, a nephew of the Wetherills, had long experience outfitting on the Navajo Reservation and in Mesa Verde. He later became the chief park ranger in Mesa Verde.

Following World War II, three returning veterans, Emmett Koppenhafer, Clifford Coppinger and Joe Rumburg re-established the horse concession. The horses had scattered across the mesa top so Coppinger, who had been an Air Force pilot, leased a large two-engine airplane to find them. He flew very low over the mesa looking for stray horses, much to the consternation of park officials.

Horses were allowed to graze on the abundant grasses of the mesa top during the off-season and were rounded up each spring, a practice that lasted well into the 1950s. When it was discontinued, having feed trucked in raised the horse concessioner's costs. In later years the horses spent winters at ranches outside the park.

Coppinger soon left Mesa Verde and established himself in the race horse business in Phoenix, Arizona. Joe Rumburg became a park ranger, worked his way up the system and distinguished himself as associate director of the National Park Service. Mesa Verde Pack & Saddle then became a true family business. Emmett and his wife Frances, a registered nurse, had had three boys, all of whom became good wranglers and farriers in the business.

Emmett was the perfect icon of his trade, born in Montezuma County to a ranch family that used horses in farming and stock-raising. He was sun-tanned and weathered, his face the mirthful embodiment of a man of the West. Emmett was a gentle person with the wit of Will Rogers. Spending a day in the saddle with him was an experience of a lifetime. Many visitors who took his trips rated it the high point of their visit. He was a master at matching horses and people. He prided himself in not having a plodding string of animals that traveled slowly along the trail like mules going down the canyon. He had spirited horses for experienced riders and gentle horses for novice riders.

The hitch rack was located just northeast of the museum on the same side of the road. Half-day and full-day trips were offered, traveling south on Chapin Mesa to several small ruins such as Casa Colorado, Two Story House and others on Navajo Canyon rim. The wranglers had a great chance to talk with riders about the plants and animals of the pinion-juniper forest and canyon rim, as well

Emmett Koppenhafer at his hitch rack in Morefield Campground.

Ted Koppenhafer

as the life of the Ancestral Puebloans.

In the early 1960s the National Park Service required Emmett to move his entire operation to Morefield Canyon, adjacent to the new campground. Two trails were established, one around the old Knife Edge Road and the other up onto the mesa between Prater and Morefield canyons. It was a good ride for people who had been in the car all day, but it was never a replacement for the great trips on Chapin Mesa. In the 1970s the park service decided horseback tours were inappropriate and Emmett was ordered to move out. Sadly, this family business that had been built with sweat equity had no "possessory interest" as the Mesa Verde Company did in its facilities and operations. After 30 years (1947-1977) taking people on horseback rides in the park, the Koppenhafers had to leave with only their horses and mobile home.

This was not the National Park Service's finest hour. There was no recognition of all of Emmett's contributions – the times when he packed water to firemen in the field; the time he stood shoulder-to-shoulder with a park ranger who had been attacked by a group of men, saving the ranger's life. There was no recognition of Frances' nursing activities with park people, no farewell party.

Soon after leaving the park, Emmett suffered a debilitating stroke. Several years later, Joe Rumburg, who had retired as NPS deputy director, went to Washington and "raised hell" about the manner in which the NPS had handled the termination. As a result, the Koppenhafers received a small cash award.

We proposed a fleet of buses to make a trip every 30 minutes on the hour and half-hour from the new Far View Visitor Center to the Wetherill parking lot. At Wetherill a minibus train would transport visitors between the stops. Environmentally this would provide a safe and quiet experience. It was agreed that the Mesa Verde Company would buy and maintain all of the equipment and that the national park would pay a flat transportation fee for a period of three years.

The company began planning a temporary food and supply facility on Wetherill Mesa. Everything would have to be hauled on the buses from Far View each day.

Vehicles posed a problem, because the road had one hill with a 17 percent grade. The average highway bus can make the grade if it is in good condition, running in low gear and driven by a driver who knows the hill. If the driver didn't make it, he had to back down. With a U-turn at the bottom and a 2,000-foot drop-off, some of the best bus drivers found the route nerve-wracking!

Specially built busses geared for the road provided the solution, so the company ordered three. The minitrain was a different problem because each had to be custom built, requiring a lead time of almost a year from order to delivery. A search found one in Englewood, almost new and in storage for several years. It was perfect in every dimension, very quiet, with open sides and a full public address system for the ranger naturalist. The minitrain served for many years until it was worn out. Wetherill Mesa opened on time and visitors had a great experience.

In the early 1980s a gondola lift was proposed, stretching from below the north rim of Mesa Verde to the top near Far View. From there other public transportation would take visitors to various ruins sites. The proposal would eliminate all roads into Mesa Verde. The gondola would carry people, supplies and even gravel and building materials!

The principals in the company claimed to have great experience in ski lift construction in this country and Europe. They originally made the proposal to the director of the NPS Rocky Mountain Regional Office. The director listened because Mesa Verde had a seemingly insurmountable problem stabilizing the entrance road. The two men then secretly contacted several prominent men in Cortez and invited their involvement. They wanted to secure the private land at the foot of the Mesa where a large commercial center could be developed.

I was alarmed when I heard of the plan because of the effect it would have on the Mesa Verde Company. I hired a private detective agency in Denver to investigate the two men and determine how capable they were of carrying out such a scheme. The private detective agency report came in and the entire scheme collapsed. The two Boulder men had only worked on a Poma ski lift and they had only $4,000 in assets between them!

Travel shows were an important contact point for visitors. Mesa Verde

Company did its own for awhile, then changed to a booth that we re-built for Club-20. The state of Colorado had a beautiful travel booth consisting of three fold-out sections with lighted transparencies. When it was damaged by a freight service, the state sold it to Mesa Verde Company. Restored and fitted to a custom cargo trailer, it was used in many travel shows in Anaheim, San Francisco, Denver, Dallas, Minneapolis, and Kansas City.

Mesa Verde Company maintained membership in the National Park Conference of Concessioners which Ansel had started and Roger continued so brilliantly. I became secretary of the group, making numerous trips to Washington D.C., and other key cities. On many of these trips I would load my briefcase with extra sales supplies. Once in Washington, I would catch a quick train to New York for sales interviews at key American Automobile Club Offices. Sales people seemed eager for the briefings and every trip paid off with more AAA reservations.

The publicity that was once so hard to come by became almost automatic. In late summer of 1978, Merrie and I took a special holiday with some other members of the Denver Museum of Natural History. This trip by saddle horse was into a geological area once known as Wheeler National Monument, now part of the Rio Grande National Forest, in Mineral County, Colorado, not far from Creede. It was a long trip. On the way the lady just ahead of me seemed very unsteady on her horse. I observed her for awhile and then rode up beside her just in time to see her collapse and fall from the horse. I swung out of the saddle and miraculously caught her before she hit the ground. Her horse bolted.

Other members of the party helped revive her. Soon they were able to help her back into the saddle and travel to the guest ranch. A lifelong friendship started that day. She was Olga Curtis, editor of Empire Magazine, a Sunday supplement for the *Denver Post*.

About two weeks later Olga Curtis returned to Cortez along with photographer George Crouter. They interviewed Merrie and me for a couple of days. On November 28, 1978, the two of us and our work in Mesa Verde were featured in the magazine.

Mesa Verde became a destination for European visitors. Some returned multiple times to buy Navajo rugs in Merrie's gift shops. To attract more of them, Merrie and I attended a 1978 National Association of Travel Agents meeting in Munich, Germany. While there, we traveled through Austria, Germany, and Switzerland to promote Mesa Verde. In preparation we had written letters of intention to a number of travel agents in Germany and packed an extra suitcase with the 16mm film, brochures and souvenirs.

We were really naïve about the process. We soon learned that the really big operators like Loew's Hotel threw very elaborate parties for the travel agents in Germany and even took troupes of showgirls. But it turned out well in the end. Sensing our ignorance, the agents we had written felt sorry for us. So they gathered together and threw a party for us. They liked the film and brochures. They assured Mesa Verde Company of their continued support and have continued to send visitors to Far View Lodge to this day.

In 1977, we published a new booklet on Mesa Verde and it became an immediate success. Merrie and I had formed a separate company, INTERpark, to publish our privately developed books, postcards and photographic items including films and videos.

The late 1970s were very good for us and Mesa Verde Company. The network expanded as I served on several boards and commissions, and was appointed to the Colorado Consulting Committee for the National Historic Preservation Act and the Advisory Committee to the Department of Commerce and Industry. The National Park Service asked me to be a member of the Regional Master Planning Team on Concessions, but my appointment led to an investigation by a Senate Oversight Committee. I testified in Washington, D.C., under the direction of Senator Alan Simpson of Wyoming. NPS successfully defended the appointment and this resulted in a stronger connection with the National Park Service. Over the years, I was invited by three different NPS directors to be chief of the NPS Concessions Office. But like my father-in-law Ansel Hall, I didn't want to live in Washington, D.C., so I respectfully turned down the offers.

In 1979, Mesa Verde Company was running well. All our earnings were being plowed back into the facilities, so the company had not paid its 23 shareholders a dividend since the 1957-58 seasons. Some of them, particularly third generation owners, understandably asked, "Where's the payout?" With none of the shareholders interested in managing the company it was time to sell. Any sale would have to be acceptable to the National Park Service, which seemed to favor large corporate operators with deep pockets. Small family type operations like Mesa Verde Company were falling out of favor.

A search led to ARA Services, which already was involved in Virginia's Shenandoah National Park and Alaska's Mount McKinley (now Denali) National Park. Their reputation was high in NPS. They were not the high bidder, but offered to solve a problem which had been growing in Mesa Verde Company. We had no retirement plan to take care of a number of faithful employees, some of whom had 20-plus years of service. ARA provided a retirement plan for June Hall and included all permanent employees in the ARA plan retroactive to their date of employment. A great weight was lifted from our shoulders.

Philadelphia-based ARA wanted to continue the Mesa Verde Company name and corporate structure as a subsidiary, and gave assurances that "nothing would change." I signed a three-year employment contract, and we proceeded with improvements to Far View Lodge and Spruce Tree Terrace.

Listed on the New York Stock Exchange, ARA Services, Inc., had been started by Bill Fishman and a Mr. Slater. Fishman had developed periodical and book distribution from a small business in Southern California to the largest in the nation. Mr. Slater had great restaurants in such prime locations as the top of Chicago's John Hancock building and the top of the Arco Towers in Los Angeles. Their collection of service companies and restaurants across the country garnered more than $585 million in annual sales, including stadium food services, janitor services, laundry services and all of the state park concessions in Alabama, as well as some in New York and Ohio.

It was not an entirely smooth transition, though. Every year in the fall ARA would send a team of auditors from the home office to audit the inventory-taking. With little understanding of native handcrafts, they were critical of the number of Navajo rugs remaining in the inventory. Instead, they advocated having a sale at the end of the season, selling off all of the prize display pieces that were carried over (and increased in value) each year.

In 1981 I was re-assigned to the ARA office in Philadelphia, where I negotiated a new 20-year operating contract with the National Park Service for Mesa Verde Company. The following year the tides changed when 50 of ARA Services' top managers formed a new company and bought out ARA shareholders. The company was taken off the New York Stock Exchange and functioned as a privately held company. A new young manager at Mesa Verde fired Merrie because she didn't manage the gift shops the way his mother did in Virginia. The Mesa Verde gift shop never again achieved the same sales levels.

I completed my contract with ARA Services that year, leaving us free to develop our own business, INTERpark, Inc. We converted our Mesa Verde movie to video and moved ahead developing other video programs. We published a weekly magazine called *Mesa Verde Today,* as well as narrow gauge train books, and republished two books on Mesa Verde.

In 1984 Colorado Governor Richard Lamm honored me with a state award for Lifetime Achievement in Tourism. The following year I was selected to partner with the manager of Denver Convention & Visitor Bureau at a Foremost West Sales trip to the Orient. Merrie paid her own way and joined the small group. Northwest Orient Airlines held sales programs in Japan, Korea, National Republic of China and Hong Kong. Yes, we were selling Colorado and we are still selling Mesa Verde! The park had been good to us and we wanted to put something back into the system.

9

THE FABULOUS FOUR CORNERS
1980S-2005

BY DUANE A. SMITH

Mesa Verde reached its 80th birthday in 1986 and like many a dowager, had grown finer with age. Tourists of the mid-1980s could hardly appreciate what their grandparents had endured to visit the park. They traveled to the park in comfort, ease, and speed their grandparents could not have imagined, but would have envied. Touring the park during that birthday year offered the best educational and vacation experience ever, despite the crowds.

The surrounding towns also displayed more tourist amenities than ever before – motels, hotels, restaurants, fast food stops, tourist shops, shopping centers, entertainment, and a variety of sights and activities – for young and old to see, savor and sample. Best of all, they generated more dollars for local businesses and individuals than ever before. Even the feud between Durango and Cortez mellowed as the century drew to a close, while Mancos continued to sit on the sideline.

"...THERE EXISTED MUCH TRUTH AMID THE PUFFERY OF 'FABULOUS'."

For some more distant towns, Mesa Verde now held less interest. Where they once had eagerly advertised Mesa Verde National Park, they now turned to promoting attractions closer to home. Moab, Grand Junction, Flagstaff, Salida, Farmington, and others that earlier aspired to be "gateways" looked to become destination points, not pass-through communities for travelers on their way to southwestern Colorado. Canyonlands, the Great Sand Dunes, Petrified Forest, Colorado National Monument, Canyon De Chelly, the Weminuche Wilderness, Zion and Bryce, Aztec Ruins and Bandelier national monuments, Chaco Canyon, and Lake Powell and Glen Canyon joined perennial favorite Grand Canyon as competition for the tourists' time, interest, and money.

Add to these a variety of national forests and a marvelous mélange of scenery all of which could be found within a day's drive of Mesa Verde and tourists had much to select from. Not to mention historic mining towns and the narrow gauge railroad from Durango to Silverton corralled their share of tourists. The four neighbor states continued trying to live up to their self-proclaimed title, the "Fabulous Four Corners." They offered more national parks, forests, and monuments, recreational areas, and historic sites within a few hours' drive than any other spot in the United States. So there existed much truth amid the puffery of "fabulous."

The travail had gone out of the trip to Mesa Verde unless one suffered car trouble or some individual problem. About the most aggravating situa-

A World Heritage Cultural Site

On September 8, 1978, the United Nations Educational, Scientific and Cultural Organization (UNESCO) designated Mesa Verde as a World Heritage Cultural Site, the only site in the United States to be so honored. It was placed on the World Heritage List to ensure that "world heritage properties are identified and that they obtain international recognition."

Mesa Verde proved eminently qualified to be on this list. The criteria included "works of man or the combined works of nature and of man, and areas including archaeological sites which are of outstanding universal value from the historical, aesthetic, ethnological or anthropological points of view." Mesa Verde National Park "is unique in the world" because it possesses "all of these values in one site."

Gil Wenger and Robert Lister had prepared the nomination and "formally presented it to UNESCO." Mesa Verde and the United States were now part of an international effort to hold "in trust for the rest of mankind those parts of world heritage found within its boundaries."

---

tion on the highway came with construction delays, heavy traffic, or a slow-moving vehicle on the road coming into the park. Large crowds on a hot day and long waits in line to tour one of the sites made the trip a little less pleasant and some people objected to having to secure tickets to tour two of the popular cliff dwellings. Still, these only temporarily hindered the visit.

Mesa Verde was attracting more foreign visitors than ever before. A visitor origin survey conducted in July 1980, for example, found that nearly 12 percent of the visitors came from foreign countries with more visitors from West Germany than neighboring New Mexico. They came from 31 countries, nearly 90 percent hailing from Europe. In his annual report, Superintendent Robert Hyder praised these visitors for being "very knowledgeable about Mesa Verde." They show great understanding of "why it is so important to preserve remnants of a past culture."

The park was designated a World Heritage Culture Site in 1978 by UNESCO, the first site in the United States to gain that well-deserved distinction. The designation hailed Mesa Verde as "unique in the world" for possessing all the desirable values of a World Heritage Cultural Site – historical, ethnological, anthropological, "purely aesthetic." Each nation, the designation specified, "holds in trust for the rest of mankind those parts of world heritage found within its boundaries."

Hyder felt that this "undoubtedly accounts for the increasing percentage visitation of foreign countries." This new influx presented several challenges. Some visitors possessed a very limited knowledge of English, making the need for bilingual guides and rangers extremely important for the

Mesa Verde National Park

"Roughing" it in the 1970s.

first time. It proved particularly difficult to find people who were knowledgeable in archaeology as well as a foreign language. Park brochures in German and French proved to be an easier solution and helped bridge the gap, making the visit more meaningful for people who spoke those languages.

All 50 states contributed visitors with slightly more than a quarter coming from the Four Corners neighbors. Colorado, Texas, and California ranked as the top three states, continuing the trend of previous years.

What did the tourists rate as "extremely" important park attributes that contributed to a successful Mesa Verde visit? To answer these questions, the park service conducted another survey in 1983. The top five responses clearly provided guidance for the future. Cleanliness of the park ranked number one, followed by information about the park, "clean, clean" air, self-guided tours, and ability to view ruins from the canyon rim. The museum ranked seventh and interestingly park ranger/interpreters came in ninth. On the bottom of the list languished the shuttle bus to Wetherill Mesa and the bus tour offered by the concessioner.

The air quality issue should not have amazed the park service.

Americans had become more environmentally aware and concerned than past generations. A survey in Grand Canyon produced the same results as Mesa Verde's. The once pristine views over the Four Corners' mountains, valleys, mesas, and deserts, which people so long had taken for granted, could no longer be so blithely assumed as a certainty. A variety of factors contributed to the change. Pollution from nearby coal-fired power plants ranked as the worst offender, joined by pollution from automobiles, acid rain, and population growth in surrounding counties.

Mesa Verde established an air quality monitoring system, not only for the public's perception and health, but because of the impact polluted air was having on the vegetation and archaeological sites. Pollution seriously endangered the ruins, and joined with rain and snow, particularly threatened the mesa top pueblos. The time-consuming, expensive, frustrating, and often discouraging efforts to reduce pollution had gone on for more than 20 years.

Most visitors, unless they had been in the park before the problem arose, probably saw only a haze on bad days without realizing it had not always been that way. Those sweeping views invariably caught visitors' attention, one of the natural "treats" and treasures for the tourists at any time. As far back as 1906, a report proclaimed the trail into the park "is one of the grandest and most extensive views in the country." That opinion is echoed today, despite the periodic haze.

Now, after all those years, people threatened this intangible treasure and no easy answers or solutions readily emerged. As threatening as acid rain and other pollutants were to the ruins, seasonal weather caused grief as well. In order to increase the public's understanding of Ancestral Puebloan culture, the mesa top sites had been stabilized and opened for viewing. Being buried had once protected the sites, but they now stood exposed to the elements. Protecting them with covers in the winter helped, but exposing the ruins added another factor to the ongoing struggle and cost of preserving the park while enhancing the public's visit.

Today's world crashed in on Mesa Verde and not just with pollution and overcrowding or the 1930s depression. The beautifully produced 1984 park guide warned "park visitors can be the target of professional thieves who rob locked vehicles and campsites." Among the recommendations – lock cars and take "valuables with you or leave them in a secure place." "Be sure" to report all thefts "immediately to the nearest ranger station." Such problems had not suddenly emerged, but rather had just become more daunting than they were earlier. No national park could ever be secure from the outside world.

The age-old parent and park service worry about children's safety when near canyon rims did not go away, despite park warnings and prohibitions or common sense exercised by tourists. Canyons are inviting to youngsters for viewing, climbing, and seeing how far a tossed rock goes. Neither

Mesa Verde National Park

Cross country skiing 1985. The mesa top roads remained available to skiers.

youngsters, nor anyone else, were to throw rocks or other "objects into canyons, there may be people below." The 1984 park guide further recommended that because of the altitude visits to the cliff dwellings could be strenuous and were not "recommended for persons with heart or respiratory ailments." The warnings had been unnecessary in the park's early days, when only the hardiest visitors could make the trek in to the ruins. With good roads, anyone could drive to the trail heads and hike down to a cliff dwelling, unaware of how the altitude, low humidity and summer heat might affect them on the uphill climb back to their cars. In the new world of the late 20th century, the government seemed to feel, in many cases rightly so, that what had been common sense to an earlier generation needed to be stressed to current tourists.

Other warnings became necessary as well. Natural danger still lurked in the park and people had to be careful. A young visitor from France in 1997 found this out in dramatic fashion when a mountain lion attacked him while he and his family walked along a park trail. That created quite a stir, as might be imagined.

Such dangers aside, the park service made strides to improve the public's experience on a variety of fronts. It seemed that Americans missed their television, so it came to Mesa Verde. In 1983, the Sipapu lounge installed a TV to "further serve visitors who enjoy television in the evenings." To meet government standards a few of the trails were made

This ad was produced by the Colorado Tourism Board. William Winkler worked with the ad agency to produce it in the mid-1980s.

William Winkler

accessible to wheelchairs where possible, along with some rooms in Far View Lodge. Park folders were printed in Braille and restrooms, drinking fountains and telephones were made handicapped-accessible. Designated handicap parking locations appeared, also, throughout the park. Although most visitors did not notice it, the computer also arrived and in a variety of ways touched their stay. For researchers, archaeologists, and other scholars, computers represented a great leap forward for their scholarship and excavations.

To add a further cultural dimension, the 1980s saw the introduction of the "Mesa Verde Indian Art Festival," which bridged the gap between the present and the past by bringing Pueblo people and others back to the park. That helped promote Mesa Verde in a different manner. So did the increased promotion of the park as a "winter wonderland" with its "splendid views" of the Montezuma and Mancos valleys, the La Plata Mountains, and other nearby sights "under a sparkling white mantle." All this made winter "one of the most beautiful times of the year to visit the park." Mesa Verde assured visitors that park crews plowed and sanded the roads, yet even so they were "advised to call ahead in time to check on latest conditions during inclement weather." Winter travel never equaled the summer days then or later, but the park in winter, without exaggeration, still presented a special treat.

Promotion came less now from outside sources but rather almost totally from concessioner and park service efforts. To be sure, nearby communities pitched in as always, but even they promoted other attractions as well. Mesa Verde could no longer count on an article or two per year in regional or national press, as it once could. The *Denver Post* and *The New York Times,* for instance, carried only one article each in the six years from 1979 to 1985. So many competing vacation spots and trips vied for attention that Mesa Verde could not keep pace with "new" attractions or headline grabbing stories.

Road closures due to slides and small fires flaring in the park did attract fleeting attention regionally, and temporarily hurt attendance without a long-range impact. The major fires of the early 21st century, however, repeatedly closed the park for short periods. Closures and fire did more damage to tourism and ruins than anything had before. Plans were made, prevention stressed, and crews readied, but Mesa Verde was one of the "hot" spots for lightning strikes in the whole country. Add to this the drought the region was suffering through, and trouble only awaited a spot to happen. The fires' magnitude would reveal short- and long-range impacts on tourism.

"…BLOW INTO THE PARK, CHECK OUT THE HIGHLIGHTS AND HIT THE ROAD."

For several years in the late 1980s and 1990s, the number of visitors topped 700,000, but more typically hovered in the 600,000 range. How much this meant to the two neighboring counties, La Plata and Montezuma, in financial terms is hard to calculate. Assuredly, it continually neared the $10 million level when jobs, purchases, and contracts directly related to the park were factored in with tourists' purchases for lodging, gas, and souvenirs. One possible indication of its significance came when mud slides closed the park road for a month in 1979. It was estimated that more than $1 million in tourist business was lost.

A 2001 survey found that "most park visitors were quite pleased with the experience." It also underscored a second, more disturbing fact. Most of the public spent little time at Mesa Verde as they rushed through their vacations trying to see as much as possible in as short a time as possible. The typical person spent one day in the park (only one in four spent the night), hurried to see Cliff Palace, Balcony House, or Spruce Tree House, or a combination thereof, and departed. A *Durango Herald* editorial (March 5, 2002) pointed out the obvious, that tourists "blow into the park, check out the highlights and hit the road." What about gaining an understanding of a grand civilization? Or, perhaps more important for the local economy, what did this mean to the tourist industry?

In some ways, these questions had been raised as far back as 1906.

Today's tourists characteristically do not plan to make Mesa Verde the sole destination of a vacation as they did in earlier days. It might be an important stop or it might be just the fact that they were in the neighborhood and decided to pay the park a visit. Perhaps mom and dad wanted their children to at least sample Mesa Verde before they hurried on to something the kids really wanted to see! In any case, it does little justice to understanding who lived in these canyons and mesa tops, or what occurred at Mesa Verde over the centuries, and what that says about the 21st century and its inhabitants. It does tell much about the hectic, hurried pace of American lifestyles, even on vacations.

Jean Pinkley, a longtime dedicated park ranger, made sage observations about the park she loved. Each person who visits Mesa Verde National Park should take to heart what she wrote.

> Though Mesa Verde was set aside primarily to preserve and use wisely the prehistoric manifestations, the scenery is unique, and spectacular, the animal and plant life varied and interesting, and the geology presents a good example of certain phases of earth history. Since environment played a major role in development of the culture found here, it becomes doubly important that it be interpreted.
>
> This national park commemorates and reminds us of the debt we owe to those who have gone before. It gives pause to the brash citizen who proclaims that our good way of life is the invention and the attainment of one particularly ingenious generation of Americans. It humbles our citizens into the realization that we owe so very much to all the people of all lands and all times.

She astutely pointed out the lessons to be learned from Mesa Verde, summarizing concisely the goals of the long struggle since 1906 to make this park available to all people.

It is not about communities and businesses making money, or about better roads and crowded parking lots, or about publicity and visitation numbers, nor about ease of transportation and vacation adventures. Those might seem to be topics of interest, but deeper meanings reside in the mysteries of Mesa Verde.

All that has gone on before has laid the groundwork for a better understanding and appreciation of where we have been, who we are, and why we are. The saga of Mesa Verde and its people perhaps might give a peek into the future and the residency limits in the Four Corners region. Might what happened to the Mesa Verde people happen also to other folks? That is what Mesa Verde and its history should and must tell the visitors who have spent the time and effort to reach this isolated part of the United States.

Shakespeare wrote in *The Tempest*, "What's past is prologue." Confucius stated "things that are past, it is needless to blame." Both are true. Today and tomorrow may learn from Mesa Verde's heritage.

SOURCES

Correspondence
Gil Wenger to Author, November 11, 1986.

Other
Air Pollution Effect on Parks and Wilderness Areas (Mesa Verde: National Park Service, 1984): 49, 51 & 57.

News Release, September 17, 1980, 1980 Superintendent Report, Mesa Verde archives.

Jean Pinkley, Interpretive Prospectus, April 8, 1966, Mesa Verde archives.

Program for the Ceremonies Commemorating the 75th Anniversary of Mesa Verde National Park, June 29, 1881, Mesa Verde archives.

Superintendent's Reports, 1980, 1982, 1983, & 1985, Mesa Verde archives.

EPILOGUE

A Place of National and International Interest

By Duane A. Smith

As Mesa Verde National Park approached its centennial, tourism displayed the successes of years gone by and the problems of the past, concerns of the present, and potential of the future. One is reminded of the late Jesse Nusbaum's astute observation in his 1929 superintendent's report. Of "paramount importance is the fact Mesa Verde is fast becoming a place of national and international interest." No longer, he wrote, was it merely of local interest or character, "nor do we depend on inhabitants of adjacent communities to furnish the majority of the visitors." That evidence of its national and international prominence as a tourist destination may be seen everywhere in the 21st century's early years.

The love affair with the park continues, and overcrowding marches right along with it. Projects such as Mission 66 and Wetherill Mesa attempted to alleviate overcrowding, and, in a sense, they accomplished their goal. At the same time, they made it possible for the park to accommodate even more visitors with at least a semblance of order and comfort. But new and enlarged parking lots as well as additional and better roads did not spell the answer either. They only eased the problems somewhat.

> "SIMPLY TRYING TO KEEP PACE WITH THE ESCALATING CROWDS HAS DROPPED THE PARK FURTHER BEHIND EACH YEAR."

Discussions have taken place and new plans have come forth for managing growth and popularity. Ideas have included a tramway, busses, and moving the park headquarters and museum to the park's entrance. Simply trying to keep pace with the escalating crowds has dropped the park further behind each year.

The major issue focuses on managing the park to balance visitors' use and enjoyment with preservation of the canyon and mesa top sites. Nothing novel runs through this discussion, whether the park in question is Yellowstone, Yosemite, Rocky Mountain, or Mesa Verde. Eventually, it would seem that the public must come to terms with limits on the number of daily visitors. Mesa Verde, or any other park, cannot be expected to absorb all the visitors, as it has in the past during the peak summer months. Overuse and crowding diminish tourists' appreciation and understanding of the sites and culture, and increase the threat to this precious and irreplaceable heritage.

Historian Hal Rothman has argued that tourism is the "Devil's bargain." It was not and is not the "panacea" for local and regional economic ills. It "typically fails," he argues, to meet the expectations of those communities and states that "embrace it as an economic strategy."

Amon Carter Museum

Showing kivas at Cliff Palace.

Some of his observations hold true for Mesa Verde and the surrounding region. Some do not. As mining and agriculture declined, tourism became more than a cottage industry and emerged as the economic pillar for today and the future. For Cortez, it became the replacement economy after the natural gas boom declined, with "options to suit almost any budget" of the touring public. Durango provided the same and held out more tourist opportunities and attractions, but it also had a college to undergird its economy. Mancos, where once Mesa Verde had been the only act in town, found that what the park giveth could also be taken away both by rivals and even the National Park Service. For other once self-proclaimed "gateways," Mesa Verde had become more of a fringe benefit than anything else. Still banking on tourism, these more distant towns looked closer to home for economic salvation.

Tourism, a true service economy, still renders the Four Corners region an economic colony to outside interests, whims, government policy, and the world situation. It's nothing different from years gone by, when mining and agriculture ruled the roost. Events such as the 9-11 attack on New York City in 2001 or a downturn in the economy make the area vulnerable, as tourist numbers drop, sales decrease and tax dollars dwindle. Rising gasoline prices dented travelers' wallets in 2004. So have financial or other crises in foreign countries, particularly in Europe and Japan, that kept travelers at home. Mother Nature has played a role, too, as the Mesa Verde fires showed in the early years of the 21st century, when the park had to be closed for days, even a week or longer. Since the fires, the public has seen a changed vista within the park and witnessed nature's slow start as vegetation reclaims the mesas and canyons.

If tourism declines, it affects individuals, towns, and countryside. As locals embrace tourism, they become more dependent on it and somehow have to encourage the industry to grow and prosper even more. Some people benefit more directly than others, but tourist dollars and cents trickle down to almost everybody eventually.

Tourism has changed all it touched from Main Street to the community as a whole. Visitors produce both the good – dollars and jobs – and the bad – from crowded streets to a motel-restaurant strip, and an atmosphere of catering to the touring public's whims. It also provokes grumbling among old-timers and newcomers alike, about cars, crowds, and the joys of the "good old days." All this obviously is not the fault of Mesa Verde, however. Mesa Verde has provided one of the allurements and a buck to be made, as have other attractions, among them the mountains, climate, skiing, mining towns, small town atmosphere, western image, and the narrow gauge railroad. Year-round tourism has come to stay, providing a benefit to shore up those long winter months when few tourists, in earlier years, came to the area.

A generation ago, when Mesa Verde closed for part of the year as winter settled in, a minor depression hit the local tourist business, in turn magnifying economic problems. That was yesterday when tradition focused on summer vacations. Tradition has changed. Now people travel in all seasons, although summer still continues to be the most popular and crowded time.

Mesa Verde had done much for the region, from long before it became a national park, which just multiplied the blessings. The park has provided jobs, generated promotion, created business, lured visitors (some of whom became settlers), bred interest in better roads and highways, boosted communities, and stimulated the economy in a host of other ways. At the same time, it has generated a built-in time bomb for itself – popularity, which has bred bumper-to-bumper visitation. Such crowding has threatened the heritage and culture represented in the park and raised questions about what future generations might see and do in Mesa Verde. By attracting people to southwestern Colorado, the park also has indirectly stimulated the very growth that threatens the quality of life and environment in a no longer pristine land. It has created an economy that depends on outside people, influences, and events. Locals are no longer masters of their own destinies, but that has been true since the first settlers arrived.

In the end, have the contributions outweighed the Devil's bargain? For the preservation of a treasured heritage, along with making it available to the public and educating the public about their country's southwestern heritage, the answer has to be "yes." Thanks in part to Mesa Verde National Park, the Four Corners region has become better known and accessible. The tourism it has helped generate assuredly provided a saving economic grace to southwestern Colorado in the 20th century. A Devil's bargain, yes, but considering the alternative of not having any real economic pillars except declining ones, what was a community like Cortez to do? When its very existence depends on finding a stimulus for the local economy, a community might easily bargain with the Devil and not worry about crowds, growth, loss of "innocence," shoddy tourism attractions and promotions, or a decline in quality of life.

Mancos lost. Tourism had been a Devil's bargain that glittered alluringly, then all too soon vanished. Durango played the game with more cards than its two rivals. Its greatest threat came not from too much dependence on tourism, but from growth and popularity. Tourism has helped bring this about, and Mesa Verde has contributed its share by advertising the region and bringing potential settlers who first came as visitors. All this simply changed the pace and timing. It would have happened anyway because of the attractions of the scenery, climate, college, outdoor lifestyles, and amenities within the community.

What, then, is the role of Mesa Verde in the region, and the region's role in park affairs? Inherent within all this are those problems and accomplishments discussed throughout this book. Perhaps the answer lies within each person and what he or she wants to see, to do, to enjoy, and perchance to decide where to live. No matter how much one might want to go back to a simpler, less crowded era, it is an impossible fantasy. Change has been part of Mesa Verde's legacy past, present, and undoubtedly in the future as well. Conceivably, too, Mesa Verde's story has something else to tell the future.

It is believed the Ancestral Puebloans were compelled to leave their

Mesa Verde cliff dwellings centuries ago because they had exhausted the natural resources of the area. At the same time, prolonged drought made water too scarce for them to continue to live and grow crops there. The parallel is clear, and the choices to be made are critical. Overcrowding and a decline in natural resources may guide a civilization down the wrong path or toward the wrong choices. We can love a park and a land to death.

Abraham Lincoln, during the dark days of December 1862, reminded his fellow citizens who held the power to save the Union. By substituting Mesa Verde National Park for the Union, his words ring as true today as they did then. "We know how to save [Mesa Verde National Park]. The world knows we do know how to save it. We, even we here, hold the power and bear the responsibility." The future will judge us on how we meet that responsibility.

SOURCES
Books
Rothman, Hal, *Devil's Bargains* (Lawrence; University Press of Kansas, 1998): 127, 158, 360, & 368-70.

Articles
Blodgett, Peter, "Selling the Scenery," *Seeing and Being Seen* (Lawrence: University of Kansas Press, 2001): 290-91.

Limerick, Patricia, "Seeing and Being Seen," *Seeing and Being Seen*, 46-47.

Pitcaithley, Dwight, "A Dignified Exploitation," *Seeing and Being Seen*: 310.

Rothman, Hal, "Shedding Skin and Shifting Weight," *Seeing and Being Seen*: 100, 108, 112, 118-19.

Other
Jesse Nusbaum, "Superintendent Report, 1929," Mesa Verde Archives: 6.

INDEX

A

AEC 127
Aileen Nusbaum Hospital 77
Air quality 171-172
Airplane 89, 131
Alamo Ranch 7, 10, 22-23
Albright, Horace 62-64
Allein, Ina 34
American Association of Museums 109
Anderson, Eva 45
Anderson, George 74
Animas City 3, 5
Ansel Hall Pueblo 113
ARA Services 164-165
Associated Grocers of Colorado 152
Auto camp 75
Auto caravans 118
Auto vacation 87
Aztec, New Mexico 124

B

Bar W chuck wagon 154
Becknell, William xvi
Birdsall, William 9

C

Cahone, Colorado 112
Campfire talks 63, 138
Canvas cottages 150
Cars 55-62, 71, 74-76, 80, 89
Cat 57, 79
Chapin, Frederick 8, 22, 29-30
Chicago World's Fair 7
Civilian Conservation Corps 86-87
Cliff Palace 6
Club-20 119, 148
Coin-operated showers 150
Colorado xvii,
    Southwest image 3-6, 8-10
Colorado Cliff Dwellings Association 13

Colorado Consulting Committee for the
    National Historic Preservation Act
    164
Colorado Historical Society 7
Concessions Policy Act of 1963 135
Conference of National Park
    Concessioners 119, 148
Cortez 21, 25, 31, 35, 124, 129,
    130, 182
Cortez Lions Club 152
Cowling, Fred 10
Coze, Paul 104
Crime 172
Crinkle Edge 9
Curry, John 26
Curtis, Olga 163

D

Day, Dave 34
Daylight-saving time 140
Delgado, Manuel 157
Denver 83
Denver & Rio Grande Railroad 5, 23,
    27, 35, 51, 54, 63, 81, 83, 88, 148
Department of the Interior 36, 53, 55
Dog 57, 79
Dominguez xv
Durango 5, 7, 21-22, 24-25, 28-30,
    35, 44, 50, 73-74, 129-131,
    182, 184

E

Escalante xv
Explorer Scouts 112
Explorers Camp For Boys 112

F

Fabulous Four Corners 169
Far View dining room 156

Far View Lodge 148-149, 155-156
Far View menu 157
Far View Terrace 148, 158
Farmington 129
Federal Highway Act of 1916 49
Fewkes, Jesse 41-43, 48, 65
Fires 175
Fort Lewis 5, 24
Fort Lewis College 130
Frahm, Helen Wells 76
Fred Harvey Company 81
Fur Trade xvi

G

Gallup 125
Gannett, Henry 4
Garfield, James R. 43
Gift shop 158
Gold King 112
Gomez, Arthur 123, 141
Governors of Four Corners 117
Great Depression 86, 88
Guilett, Meredith 153

H

Hall, Ansel F. 87-88, 104, 109, 116-117, 134, 139
Hall, June Alexander 113-114
Hall, Roger 113, 147-148, 151
Hardacre, Emma 3
Henderson, Palmer 9
Hickman, Minnie 31
Higley, Elmer 51
Horses 57, 160
Hospital 77
Hyder, Robert 170

I - J

INTERpark 164-165
Jackson, William Henry 3, 6, 27, 96
Jeep, Fred 73
Jeep, Oddie 63
Jensen, Louisa 78-79

K

Kelly, C.B. 47, 57, 115
Kelly, Lee 25
Kids Korral 133
Knife Edge 72, 76, 100, 128-129
Koppenhafer, Emmett 115, 118, 160

L

Leonard, William 34-35
Lincoln, Abraham 185
Lister, Robert 170

M

Macomb, John xvi
Mancos 5, 10, 21-22, 28, 30-32, 35, 42, 44, 46, 53, 73, 111, 131, 184
Manitou Springs 124
Marshall, R. B. 48
Mason, Charlie 6
Mather, Stephen 62-63, 73, 76
McClurg, Virginia 12-14, 36, 60, 124
Mears, Otto 26-27
Mesa Verde Company 109-111, 118, 132, 135, 138, 152
Mesa Verde Enterprises 134
Mesa Verde Indian Art Festival 174
Mesa Verde Map & Guide 119
Mesa Verde National Park 15, 32-33, 41
    Headquarters 53, 55, 73
    International Interest 89
    Impact 21
    Problems 41-42
    Significance 176
    U.S. Government Role 33-34, 42, 49
Mesa Verde Pack & Saddle 160
Mesa Verde Park Company 83
Mesa Verde Savings and Loan Association 152
Mesa Verde Today 165
Mesa Verde Transportation Company 80, 81
Million Dollar Highway 84
Mills, Enos 54

Minibus train 162
Mining 3
Mission 66 136, 137, 139, 140, 147
Moab, Utah 86
Model T 98
Montezuma County Commissioners 117
Montrose 86
Morefield Amphitheatre 157
Morefield Campground Village 149
Morefield Canyon 148-149, 161
Morefield Village 149-150
Morgan, William 4
Moss, John 21
Motel 75
Mount Vernon 11
Mountain lion 173
Moving picture machines 50
Museum 46, 63, 77-78, 86

N

National Association of Travel Agents 163
National Geographic Society 139, 151
National Park Conference of
 Concessioners 163
National Park Movement 10-14
National Park Service 50, 62, 138
Native American arts and crafts 114
Native American handcrafts 154
Navajo Hill 148
Navajo rugs 159
Navajo Trail 147
Navajo Trail Association 117, 131
New Deal 86-87
Newberry, John xvi
Newell, F. H. 9, 11
Nina Heald Webber
 Southwest Colorado Collection 95-105
Nordenskiöld, Gustaf 7
Nusbaum, Aileen 77
Nusbaum, Deric 72
Nusbaum, Jesse 71-73, 75, 78, 83,
 125, 181

P

Pack and Saddle 149
Parrott City 3, 22-23
Parsons, Eugene 15, 54
Peabody, Lucy 13-14, 98
Pinkley, Jean 176
Point Lookout Lodge 134
Pollution 172
Possessory interest 148, 151, 155
Postcards 95
Promotion 50-52, 54, 83, 116, 119,
 123, 131, 158, 162-163, 174

R

Radio 83, 84
Railroads 9, 26, 52, 75
 see also Denver & Rio Grande
 Railroad and Rio Grande Southern
 Railroad
Rainbow Bridge/Monument Valley
 Expedition 109, 112
Rainbow Route 27
Randolph, Hans 41-43
Rickner, Esma 53
Rickner, Thomas 49, 55, 84
Rio Grande Southern Railroad 8, 26-28,
 35, 54, 116
Road problems 81, 175
Roads 42-44, 46, 49-50, 58, 71,
 123-126
Rockefeller, John D., Jr 77
Rocky Mountain National Park 83
Roosevelt, Franklin 86
Roosevelt, Theodore 14, 34, 36
Ross, Kenneth 112
Rothman, Hal 181
Rumburg, Joe 160

S

S.W. Colorado image 84
Saddle Lectures 118
Santa Fe Railroad 81
Santa Fe Transportation Company 81

Sipapu Bar 132, 157, 173
Smiley, Emory 47
Spanish xv
Spanish Trail Association 52
Spruce Tree Camp 79
Spruce Tree Lodge 110-111, 116, 132, 148
Spruce Tree Terrace 154

Wirth, Conrad 139
Wolf Creek Pass 60-61, 76, 125, 127
Women 11-14
World Heritage Cultural Site 170
World War I 64-65
World War II 89

T

Television 131
Thomas, Chester A. 151-152
Thomas, Sterl 31
tour busses 159
tourist advice 53

U

University of California at Berkeley 109
Uranium 126-127
Ute Mountain Utes 13
Ute War 5

V

Vanderhoof, John 158
Victorian women 10
Visitors' center 140

W

Wade, Jack 160
Wadleigh, Frank 52
Water 46-48, 76, 133-134
Watson, Don 115, 118
Wenger, Gil 170
Wetherill Mesa 139, 162
Wetherill Mesa Archaeological Project 136
Wetherill, Benjamin 5
Wetherill, John 110
Wetherill, Louisa Wade 110
Wetherill, Richard 6, 8
Wetherills 7, 22
Winkler, Merrie Hall 114, 116, 147, 152

Sources of Mesa Verde postcards used in this book

The postcards used in chapter 5 were selected and used by permission of the Center of Southwest Studies. They all are from Volume 3 of the postcards in Collection M 194, the Nina Heald Webber Southwest Colorado Collection at the Center of Southwest Studies, Fort Lewis College.

The home page of the Webber postcards descriptions online is http://swcenter.fortlewis.edu/inventory/PostcardsInv.htm

Collection, volume, and item number	URL for viewing on the Web
M1943001F	http://swcenter.fortlewis.edu/images/M194/M1943001FPage.htm
M1943002F	http://swcenter.fortlewis.edu/images/M194/M1943002FPage.htm
M1943003F	http://swcenter.fortlewis.edu/images/M194/M1943003FPage.htm
M1943004F	http://swcenter.fortlewis.edu/images/M194/M1943004FPage.htm
M1943007F	http://swcenter.fortlewis.edu/images/M194/M1943007FPage.htm
M1943014F	http://swcenter.fortlewis.edu/images/M194/M1943014FPage.htm
M1943018F	http://swcenter.fortlewis.edu/images/M194/M1943018FPage.htm
M1943030F	http://swcenter.fortlewis.edu/images/M194/M1943030FPage.htm
M1943036F	http://swcenter.fortlewis.edu/images/M194/M1943036FPage.htm
M1943040F	http://swcenter.fortlewis.edu/images/M194/M1943040FPage.htm
M1943044F	http://swcenter.fortlewis.edu/images/M194/M1943044FPage.htm
M1943048F	http://swcenter.fortlewis.edu/images/M194/M1943048FPage.htm
M1943053F	http://swcenter.fortlewis.edu/images/M194/M1943053FPage.htm
M1943055F	http://swcenter.fortlewis.edu/images/M194/M1943055FPage.htm
M1943057F	http://swcenter.fortlewis.edu/images/M194/M1943057FPage.htm
M1943068F	http://swcenter.fortlewis.edu/images/M194/M1943068FPage.htm
M1943089F	http://swcenter.fortlewis.edu/images/M194/M1943089FPage.htm
M1943095F	http://swcenter.fortlewis.edu/images/M194/M1943095FPage.htm
M1943112F	http://swcenter.fortlewis.edu/images/M194/M1943112FPage.htm
M1943200F	http://swcenter.fortlewis.edu/images/M194/M1943200FPage.htm

To request the use of any of any images in collections at the Center of Southwest Studies, for reproduction by any means, for any purpose, please complete Image Duplication Request Form that is available online at http://swcenter.fortlewis.edu/Info_researchers/sw-4.htm